It Takes Moxie

Off the Boat, or Out of School, to Making It Your Way in America

It Takes Moxie

Off the Boat, or Out of School, to Making It Your Way in America

Maureen Francisco

It Takes Moxie

ISBN: 978-1-935723-65-3

Printed in the United States of America

First Printing: 2012

CONTENTS

To my mom for believing in me and to anyone with a dream.
Let this book help you believe you can turn your
heart's desire into a reality.
You just need *Moxie*.

Acknowledgments

This country will continue to prosper as long as immigrants are welcomed here. In this book I hope I've provided good advice and helpful hints for immigrants and those new to the workplace on how to succeed in America in today's economy. Immigrants with their work ethic and new graduates with their ideas are vital to our economy. They don't take away jobs, but rather provide opportunities for us all.

As an immigrant to this country and as a woman, I have seen how hard work and application can break down barriers and provide great opportunities. By learning the language, getting an education, being dogged and resourceful, and opening new doors when others closed, I was able to achieve my American Dream. The same is possible for everybody, whatever your nationality, whatever your circumstances, if you are willing to "make it happen."

Before I begin with the long list of people I wish to thank, first, I want to thank God. None of my success, even this book, would have happened if it weren't for the grace and guidance of my Higher Power.

To Mom: You've sacrificed so much and have always given me unconditional love. You always told me to pray and think positive. Throughout my childhood, I remember you constantly telling me to reach for the stars. As an adult, your words permeate my thoughts every day. Thank you for always being in my corner. One day, when I become a mom, I only hope I can be as unselfish as you.

Thank you, Lola and Grandma Mary. Both of you are women who survived trying times and became successful. Through your example, Lola, you've shown me the importance of always working hard to fulfill your obligations. And Grandma Mary you've shown me how to be an independent woman and fiscally responsible.

Thank you, Catherine, my childhood friend, for being such a strong woman, and "Jlee" for bringing out the inner child in me and being available for those late-night talks.

My mentor Dr. Connie Mariano took me under her wing and has helped me spread mine. I'm flying. Thank you!

I thank Linda Konner, my hard-working literary agent, for giving me a chance and championing my voice. You knocked on so many doors, and when we heard a no, you believed in me and kept knocking until we heard a yes from a publisher.

Thank you, Justin Sachs of Motivational Press, for believing in my voice and message by publishing my book.

John Nelson, thank you for being that second set of eyes. This journey is one I will remember fondly as you helped me with your superb editing. You have been an excellent writing coach by challenging me at the right times and praising me when I needed it the most. This has been a great working relationship that allowed me to grow as a writer and a person. Thanks for being part of my team.

To all the people I've interviewed for this book: If it weren't for you, this book would not be possible. Even though my readers can't meet you in person, I hope that I captured the life lessons you taught me so your wisdom will now carry on to others.

To James Tabafunda, thank you for your unconditional support when I needed a friend to get me through my writing block.

To David Van Maren, thank you for being an excellent mentor and constantly reminding me of my potential. You know how to pat my back yet push me enough to always go the extra distance.

To Ron Chew, RobRob, Marie Heaney, Erin Looby, and Steve Gee, thank you for reviewing my manuscript.

Thank you, Ruben Malazo Jr., for helping me build my platform through your technical expertise.

Thank you, Robert Galinsky, for always thinking of me when it comes to your many projects, and Valerie Smaldone for including me on your team and coaching me along the way.

And to all of you for taking the time to be part of the most amazing journey of my life to date and helping me fulfill a lifelong dream, thank you! I wish you much success on your dreams.

FOREWORD

By Dr. Connie Mariano
Former Physician to the President of the United States and Director of the White House Medical Unit

When I was first introduced to Maureen Francisco by a colleague and heard a little of her immigrant story, I was amazed by the similarity of our Filipino backgrounds and our mutual drive to succeed. I can remember well when my navy steward father was transferred to Hawaii and I only spoke the Filipino dialect of Pampanga, and I had to quickly learn English, like Maureen, by watching television and mouthing the words spoken by news commentators and actors.

Like Maureen, I resolved at an early age that if I were to succeed in my new country, I needed to speak English better than my Anglo classmates. I also know of the prejudice she encountered in school because of her foreign background before she mastered the language. There are many hard lessons that immigrants of any generation face when they come to America. And they don't get any easier as you climb the ladder to success. When I told people I was in the navy, they assumed I was enlisted and not an officer. When I told them I was in the health care profession, they assumed I was a nurse and not a doctor. In fact, a new aide at the White House once ordered me to fetch water for the president, because I was Filipino, not realizing I was the president's doctor and not his valet.

This is why it's such a pleasure to write the foreword to this wonderful and timely book about how to succeed in America, one I wished I had had to guide me on my own journey a generation earlier. Whether one has just stepped off the boat or off "the Boeing," has just graduated from college or is looking for a new job or career, any reader will find excellent step-by-step advice on how to make it in the new workplace.

America is indeed, as it proved for me and my family, a place of great opportunity. But it is also a place with few entitlements, especially for immigrants. For the most part, hard work and dedication will pay off. Not everybody can be a Donald Trump—although I am amazed by the number of millionaire immigrants whose stories are told here—but with enough moxie, of which Maureen has plenty, following the guidelines in this excellent book, you can make your way and find your place in the sun.

PREFACE

In July 2007, I found myself in an interview with a room full of network executives, producers, and writers—twenty or so people—staring at me and hanging on to my every word. They were interviewing me to be on a reality show called *Solitary 3.0* for the FOX Reality Channel.

It had been a lifelong dream of mine to get on a reality show after watching the first season of *Survivor.* I loved the drama, the competition, and "the great lengths to which people would go" for one million dollars.

Six years later, after sending out countless audition tapes and filling out applications from my credit history to questions like "Who would you want to be stranded with on a deserted island?" (I picked Jennifer Lopez, as that woman cannot escape the paparazzi, and we know *they* can find anyone), I was just one question away from cracking the code and finally getting on a reality show.

"So, Maureen, why do you think you should be on *Solitary* and what skills do you possess to make you the ultimate winner?" asked one of the network executives. There were five men—all white—among the others cross-examining me. "To be honest with you, you look a bit high maintenance to be on this show."

I leaned back and crossed my legs, letting that question sink in. He was right. By my appearance alone, I looked as if I belonged on some fashion show. I was wearing my silk brown short-sleeved blouse and tan capri shorts with brown high-heeled boots that came up to my knees. My hair was perfectly curled, long and flowing, and my makeup done for the camera. I certainly didn't look like a candidate for a show where I would find myself in a pod, isolated from any human contact, cell phones, and technology and deprived of sleep, showers, and food for long periods of time. The only way to leave the show is if you are the first contestant to quit during a challenge, but since you're alone in a pod, you have no way of knowing who threw in the towel first. It's a show about you competing against yourself.

"You're right. I'm someone who likes to get their Starbucks each morning, enjoy my manis and pedis, and indulge myself at the spa. I'm a girl who loves to be pampered. But, it hasn't always been that way."

My eyes canvassed the room and I had all twenty people absorbed in my moment. "You'd never guess, but I used to share a house that had only one bathroom with fifteen family members. At night, we'd turn the living room into our bedroom. We'd sleep on the cold, cement floor. Rats—the size of cats—would scamper past us scavenging for food. If I close my eyes, I can still smell the open sewer. This was all my family had ever known until we immigrated to America when I was five years old. At that age, I saw why my mother wanted us to come here . . . to have a real life."

As I told my story, I looked each person in the eye. "It did not discourage me when my parents didn't have the money to send me to the college of my choice. I worked my butt off at three jobs and became a well-rounded student so I could apply for scholarships and grants, which ended up paying three-fourths of my college education. When I learned there was a slim chance of getting a TV reporting job right out of college, I spent my spring break meeting with news directors across the Northwest. I was the only one in my graduating class to be offered several on-air positions, and had a five-year TV reporting and anchoring career all over the country—one in the top twelve market, Seattle. When my fiancé broke up with me after eleven years as a couple, I used that hurt to run four marathons in one year. When I got the reality show bug six years ago, I kept sending in audition tapes and only heard years of NO's. Heck no! And, no way! I've earned everything in my life. This show is more about mental toughness than physical strength. Life has prepared me for *Solitary 3.0.*"

I didn't get applause from my audience, not even a smile. The people at the audition just showed poker faces, and I had no clue if I would be a contestant on the show. I got *nothing*.

Well, a few days later I got a phone call from one of the casting directors who told me to pack my bags. I was expected to be on set in just a few days. I was selected from among thousands of applicants to be one of ten contestants. I'd applied previously to be on the show, but this time I finally got in. "Maureen, you've got moxie. Congratulations on getting on *Solitary 3.0.*"

I learned a very important lesson. Nobody cared about my immigrant poverty story until that moment when I turned my life around. I didn't let my past make me a victim. Instead, I used my past as motivation for what I don't want my future to look like.

And, I have so many people to thank, whom I'll introduce throughout the book, especially Mom. She consistently encouraged me to keep envisioning what I wanted my future to look like and reminded me I could be anything I wanted to be: a model, an actor, a reporter, a reality show star, and an executive. Anything! Soon, I started to drink the Kool-Aid too and believed in my own unlimited future.

So, this book will explore how *you* too can have anything you want. It begins with me introducing you to certain life skills, among them: Accountability, Assertiveness, and Great Attitude. If you haven't met them, you'll get to know them very well indeed.

What do you want out of life? Is it to provide for your family? Are you receiving government assistance and you'd like to be able to stand on your own two feet without any help? Do you want to send your children to college? Do you want to go to college yourself? What's missing from your current situation that's preventing you from being truly happy? What skills are you lacking that are keeping you from getting the job you want? Do you want to improve your English? Would you like to learn how to drive a car and be able to travel at your leisure? We'll write our goals down and create an action plan to help you live the life you've always wanted, be the person you always wanted to be, and find out what it takes to get the job done.

Throughout the book, I am going to be injecting "aha" moments or "life lessons" I've learned. They are the *Cliffs Notes* of my life that have helped me get ahead, which I know you'll find useful. Some of these lessons I've learned from others, and some were self-taught and learned the hard way. While my book is based on true events, the names of some individuals and/or places may have been changed to protect and give privacy to those I've written about.

As you're reading this intro, you may have asked yourself, "Who is she to write this book? What gives her the credentials to be giving advice? Why should I listen to her?"

Those are good questions. I'd be asking those very same questions myself.

Well, I am your typical immigrant who came to this country in a family who wanted to have a piece of the American Dream. But, what sets my story apart is that I not only dreamed the dream, I had a plan for achieving my goals and working my way to the top. Today, you can find me online, on TV, on the radio, and even in print, either talking about reality shows or inspiring people to live up to their best potential. I'm not Martha Stewart, but I'm what you can be in whatever endeavor you choose, with the right "moxie."

So, let's not ever forget, I am just like you. I didn't come from a rich family. I didn't get a Harvard MBA. I didn't receive inheritance money. I came from nothing, yet that didn't discourage me from dreaming and believing in myself. Life made me work hard to turn my visions into something tangible. My success came with pain and lots and lots of rejections. For every door that slammed in my face, I went knocking on the next because I knew it was just a matter of time before one would open. I. Never. Stopped. Believing.

I wouldn't allow anyone to tell me otherwise, as he or she didn't know the journey I've taken. My past is something I often reflect upon, but never dwell on. I can appreciate my humble beginnings, where my family lived in the shanties of Manila. Fear for our next meal, when the bills would be paid, and how to make ends meet were always in the forefront of Mom's mind. She later told me this so that I'd never take my blessings for granted. I could only imagine the anxiousness she felt, carrying the responsibility for fifteen family members on her shoulders. My mother didn't have time to let life defeat her. I never saw her pull out the "victim" card or tell the "woe is me" story. She had a burning desire to succeed. Failure wasn't an option. And, she passed that type of mentality onto me.

So when I immigrated to America at the age of five, I spoke very little English. Unable to express myself to my peers, I remember they were cruel with their words and actions. I fell behind in school, and the district transferred me to another school that specialized in students like me who spoke English as their second language. At home, my stepfather created an "English-only rule" at the house so I could practice my English. On top of that, I'd watch the news to listen to how the reporters spoke English and say those very same words out loud. This wasn't a one-time occurrence, but became a regular routine in my life. I was determined to go back to my original school and show my classmates that I, too, could talk like them. They had no idea that I wouldn't be able to shut up. Who would've guessed that I'd be getting paid to talk for a living, that reporting was to be part of my future.

Fourteen years after the day I was speechless during recess and my classmates teased me, I found myself living in New York City, all-expenses paid, as a summer fellow for the International Radio & Television Society Foundation Fellowship college program. Here I was, rubbing elbows with media people who got paid to express themselves and tell stories for a living. Those included ABC and NBC correspondent Deborah Roberts, the CEO of Viacom, Inc., Sumner Redstone, and many more. I even had a glass of wine with Evander Holyfield and talked about his infamous fight with Mike Tyson (where Mike bit off a portion of his ear). Let me tell you, no one was cruel to this college girl that evening or that summer as I expressed myself, freely, uninhibited, and with confidence.

When that fellowship experience was over, I had learned the importance of not only making connections, but also treating people as human beings, not steps on a ladder. The spring break of my senior year, while my peers were "taking a break," I drove all over the Northwest meeting with news directors and dropping my résumés off and getting to know them.

When I graduated from college, I was the only one in my graduating class who received several TV reporting job offers from various stations. It reinforced what I had learned from my mother and from my own trial and error: Go the extra distance, literally, and have face-time with key decision makers. Mom did the same thing. When she was a hotel housekeeper, she "cleaned house" literally by exceeding expectations at her job. Her supervisors took notice and promoted her to catering receptionist and eventually program coordinator. She ended up leaving the hotel industry altogether and later retired from Boeing as a communications specialist.

With Mom's go-win-them-over-attitude fresh in my mind, I knew I had to start somewhere. It was the NBC affiliate in Yakima, Washington, that won me over. Yakima was a respectable-size market for an entry-level reporter at the start of his or her career. To paint the broad picture, there are 210-plus television markets across the country, and Yakima, Washington, ranks around market #120. The size of the market is based on the population of the city. And, I told myself, this move to Yakima—a rural town known more for its agriculture than city life—was only the first step. The station finished in last place in ratings, but I didn't care. I was happy to be earning a living as a TV reporter. I just knew if I worked hard, refined my storytelling skills, and made calculated career decisions, I could find myself doing this job in Seattle within five years. (I would be twenty-seven years old.) Seattle is #12 in the market. Was it a lofty goal? Yes. Doable? Yes again.

Unfortunately, my news director at the NBC affiliate didn't care about my ambitious career goals. After less than five months on the job, he let me go. My boss didn't like my accent, my storytelling, my this and that . . . I walked out of the station feeling like I had been in a fight and I had just got knocked down. Where was Evander when I needed him?

But I immediately started e-mailing my contacts and making phone calls. Thank goodness I had interviewed with nearly all the news directors in the Pacific Northwest during my spring break because most remembered me. In less than twenty-four hours after hearing the words "You're fired" at the third-place station, the #1 station in the same market said, "You're hired." The CBS affiliate was about to launch its weekend newscast and needed help. I accepted the reporting position. Right then, I could hear my former news director's jaw drop to the floor.

My participation with the launch of the weekend newscast helped the station receive a #1 rating for its brand-new shows, leaving my old station in the dust. A year later, the station promoted me to be its weekend anchor and producer. And I was on my way.

CHAPTER ONE

The No-Excuse Zone

"We'd like you to start on Monday," my news director said.

"Great! See you then. I won't let you down," I said.

As I hung up the phone, I could see my name flash across the television screen reporting live at the scene of a breaking news story. Finally, my childhood dream to be a reporter would come to fruition in less than seventy-two hours. Oh wait. That's in three days.

And, then, reality hit me. Did I have enough time to pack my things? Where was I going to live? How was I going to get there? I hadn't thought about the logistics of what it was going to take to move my life to the other side of the mountains. When he called, I could've asked for a week to move, but I agreed to be there ready to work in three days.

Follow Through on Your Agreements

I wanted to panic, but there was no time. I certainly couldn't call back my news director and tell him that I needed more time to pack my belongings, get an apartment, and buy a car. If I now asked for more time to make the move, it might have sounded like I was making excuses to him, or that I didn't think things through before making commitments.

I didn't want to make excuses because life didn't exactly go my way, but find a way to get around those roadblocks. If I told my news director I wouldn't be able to make the move, it might have also planted the seed in his head that I couldn't meet deadlines. He expected me to be at the station ready to do my job in three days, and I agreed to that deadline. It was like him saying "I want your story in the can on my desk by 4:00 P.M." The details of how I was going to move to Yakima weren't his problem. They were mine, and I had to assume responsibility for them.

My news director had fulfilled his job: find a reporter to fill the opening news slot. Now, I had to do my job: make sure I came to the station ready to work on the agreed-upon date.

If I told him I just wasn't ready to make the move and needed more time, I could've been replaced. We're all replaceable, especially in the news business or for most jobs where we haven't established credibility.

So, I managed my anxiety and reminded myself I had everything under control. I had the means to pack my belongings, with my family willing to help. I had a lead on a vacancy at an apartment building in town, and I had the resources to buy a car. I had to execute my moving plan immediately and without excuses. I had to get my butt in gear.

The following day, I went to a car dealership. I had to buy a car that day as my 1983 Dodge Colt was on its last legs. It would constantly fail to start. Mom and I were both worried the car would stall somewhere in the middle of the mountain pass. She knew I needed reliable transportation. So, she volunteered to cosign with me on the car with the expectations I would be paying for the monthly payments and insurance.

I bought a black four-wheel-drive Toyota RAV4 with tinted windows, CD player, and sunroof. It called my name. The following day, I drove to Yakima in my new SUV with the trunk filled with clothes and my TV. Since the RAV4 had plenty of "junk in the trunk," I called her Beyoncé. My parents followed in their truck, which carried my rollaway bed, dresser, and kitchen table.

I learned from my news director that the main news anchor's apartment building had a vacancy.

"The laundry room is in the basement of this building. It costs just seventy-five cents each," the property manager told me. "You'll also find plenty of storage space down there. The dumpster is in the back parking lot. The mailbox is at the very front of the building."

I looked around the quaint but small studio apartment, where paint chips were peeling off the walls. The studio certainly had character, with a walk-in closet and a clawfoot bathtub. I preferred to live in a newer building with amenities like a gym and a swimming pool, but I didn't have the time to canvass the city for other apartments. And, I had learned from my news director that these studios were the most inexpensive ones in the city. My salary didn't resemble Barbara Walters's. My other option was to stay at a hotel. But that would cause a problem: where would I put my furniture? If my main anchor had been living there for more than a year, the place couldn't be that bad. I had a solution right in front of me.

Do What It Takes to Move Forward

"I'll take it," I said and opened up my checkbook.

Securing the first apartment I saw cost me the quietness and the sleep I so desperately needed. I lived on the second floor and could hear my neighbors all around me. My anxiousness for the first day at work acted as a natural alarm clock. I got ready in plenty of time. With the station located less than three miles away, I walked into the station with fifteen minutes to spare before the 8:00 A.M. meeting.

"Great to see you, Maureen," my news director said. "Let me introduce you to everyone . . ."

I finally let out a sigh of relief. I certainly didn't let my news director down and came to work on time as agreed. It wasn't necessary to share with him the great lengths I went through to make sure I reported to work on the first day. He may have cared, but it really didn't matter. All he cared about was for me to show up on time. In the end, it's all about executing and not making excuses.

NO EXCUSES—Those two words should be permanently tattooed in your brain. Excusing yourself for being late to work, missing deadlines, failing to execute because of this or that excuse will be a roadblock to keeping your job, or getting a better one, or achieving your dreams. Each day you show up at your job or jobs, meet with business contacts, or conduct yourself around others, you are sending a message on how you want to be viewed. Do you want to be seen as someone who is dependable, a real go-getter able to get the job done? If you do, you have to fix whatever prevents you from "showing up."

Others See You the Way You See Yourself

You will be seen as unreliable if you are late for work, miss work, or miss critical deadlines. People will start losing faith in you. For every shortcoming you have, others will be magnified more or even imagined. Before you know it, you're out the door; or if this is how you see yourself, it will show up in job interviews and you'll never get in the door. Look at yourself, look at your history, and fix it. If that takes counseling, get it.

This reminds me of when I was anchoring, reporting, and producing the news in Savannah, Georgia. There was a reporter who often missed her deadlines, and the producers often had to float her story to the next block of the show. Let me tell you that it got old really quick. Photographers started requesting to not go out on stories with her because they got frustrated editing the footage at the last minute. The anchors and producers would never give her the "lead" or "top story," fearing she couldn't deliver at the top of the hour. Managers stopped "investing" in her and used their energy mentoring and coaching other reporters.

She always had a reason (excuse) for why she missed her deadline: equipment failure, or the interview cancelled, or there wasn't enough time to run the story, or she couldn't find a story at the location, and so on. She earned the reputation as undependable, unreliable, and unpredictable, not just in our newsroom, but every newsroom in that market. The news business is small. That reporter eventually found herself without references for her next job. The last time I heard, she had left the news business. It's a shame; she had ability, but she just couldn't "show up."

So, this is a time for you to look at your current situation and ask yourself the following questions: What's my reputation at work? Among my friends and family? Among casual acquaintances or even strangers on the street? Am I seen as dependable? Or undependable? If it's the latter, it's time to clean up your act right now before your behavior costs you your job, your promotion, or your next job. What's making you late for work? Is it because you can't wake up on time? You don't have reliable transportation? You don't have trustworthy childcare? Please!

Why are you *not* performing at your job? Do you need more coaching and guidance? Is it because you don't have the skill set to execute the expectations of the job? Do you not like your boss? What is it? Could it be because of your past—you were born into poverty? You didn't have parents who supported you? You came from another country, and you can't speak English? You couldn't afford to go to college? I am not trying to be insensitive. But, when you "package" why you can't do something, you are simply making excuses and taking on the "victim mentality." Frankly. No. One. Cares. You've got to STOP making excuses now. Whatever it takes, fix it.

We Are the Excuse

You want to figure out the problems or attitudes that are creating the excuses you're making before someone else comes up with the solution for you, like showing you the door or closing it in your face. Because guess what . . . others also have their own problems to deal with and they are *not* bringing them into the workplace. Leave your personal life at home. Take a good look at yourself, and figure out why you're behaving in ways that hurt you, your family, and your future. Show up at work with your A-game, or your "game face," as they say.

Over time, missing one or two days of work could compound into something worse, with your employer *completely* losing faith in you and just cutting you loose. Now your personal problems have been intensified. How are you going to pay your bills? Will you lose your apartment or house? Do you think your landlord or the bank will understand your situation? Don't you think that he/she/they have bills or employees that need to be paid, too? What about your car? How do you explain to your future employer why you lost your job? How are you going to feed your family and/or your dog or cat?

Then, the psychological effects start warping your mind when you don't have control of your situation. When I procrastinated starting my college term papers, I didn't produce the best writing. Staying up late and pouring down cups of coffee and pulling all-nighters wore me down. So, I stopped putting myself into that vicious cycle, knowing very well I didn't like the consequences or results—poor grades. I promised myself I would never wait until the last minute again to write my paper because in the end, I would just hurt myself. Since my scholarships were dependent upon achieving good grades, I fixed the problem right away with better time management. Each day, I set aside time to write my paper so that I had a chance to get feedback from my professors on whether I was on course with the project. When I turned in my paper, I knew I had hit the mark and could expect good results.

Stand Out In a Good Way

When you don't make excuses, even if you're late on the job or with an assignment and immediately correct it, others will want you to be part of their team. Why? Because you've got a get-it-done, don't-complain attitude.

For example, take the story of the president and CEO of Mega Pacific Investments, Ltd., a financial and international consulting firm based in Seattle. He is a strong believer that excuses get you nowhere in life. I met Jesse Tam at a gala dinner for a nonprofit organization called Ascend, where I sit on the board. Ascend's goal is to help cultivate today's and tomorrow's Pan Asian American. I learned Jesse is an immigrant himself who bought a one-way ticket from Hong Kong to Twin Falls, Idaho, with only three hundred dollars in his pocket. At seventeen years old, he wasn't satisfied with his current situation and desired to seek another life where no one looked like him, spoke like him, or had the same background. He found it in Idaho.

Within one week, he got a job making pizzas. Jesse knew that staying in America required that he take on a job right away to pay for his way through college and living expenses. It was his choice to seek independence away from his parents and be an adult. So, Jesse needed to act like one. He couldn't call his parents and say he was short on cash. He had brought this new life upon himself.

After two years, Jesse moved to a bigger city—to Boise, Idaho. "I never stopped working. I never stopped learning. Every summer, I would take on more of a full-time job. I did more different types of jobs in those four years than at any other time in my life, from bussing tables, to being a door-to-door salesman, to working at radio stations and libraries, to doing auto repair—anything you can dream."

So, when Jesse graduated from college, he was ready to take on a "white-collar job." Because of his survival instincts and amazing work ethic, five companies offered him a position. Jesse took the management-trainee job at First Security Bank of Idaho. He felt this position would give him the best education possible for someone right out of college. But, he forgot to ask one very important question, "When does the position start?"

"But the program would not start for another six months and I couldn't last for that long. I had to pay rent, and I had to buy gas for my car." So, Jesse asked if the bank could give him another job until then. He was told to come in on Monday morning, and the bank would figure something out.

Jesse said, "So, I went in on Monday morning with my new shirt, new tie, and new suit ready to become a banker and was sent all the way down to the mailroom in the basement. As far as I was concerned, it was the most degrading job that I had ever had. I was so embarrassed that I couldn't tell my family."

Rather than sulk, Jesse found a way to make the job interesting and educational. "One of the things I learned at that time was whatever I do, I will do my best. Whatever I do, I will learn something new about that." Jesse took it upon himself to learn how to pronounce the employees' names he saw on the envelopes. Soon his colleagues throughout the bank were impressed with Jesse's ability to know everybody's name and position. So, by the time he entered the management-trainee program, he stood out in a good way. People told him, "This guy is one of the most outstanding trainee participants we've ever had. He demonstrates a personality that connects with people." Jesse said that is one of the most crucial elements a person could utilize in life in order to be successful—how to connect with people.

That job was the beginning of a career in the banking world that would span more than thirty years.

This is somewhat similar to when I applied for the sales account executive position at an online marketing company for real estate agents called Market Leader Inc. I had no sales experience in this business, but the decision maker hired me based on my ability to meet deadlines as a reporter and the testimonials my references gave to me for my dependability.

At my new company, I worked hard, extremely hard, putting in long hours and working most weekends. I didn't want the hiring managers to second-guess their decision to hire someone without a sales background.

Instead, I exceeded their expectations. During my second full month with the company, I finished as the sixth top producer in the company and earned an all-expenses paid trip to Cabo San Lucas with my mother.

And, I kept producing the same results month after month. The executives of the company came to know me not as just an employee in cubicle G, but by my name. I stood out among hundreds of sales people. It was evident that my ability to bring in sales for the company was making a name for me. The trainers would have newbies sit next to me and listen to my pitches. I learned quickly that if I did good work, or showed up high on their sales reports, people would take the time to get to know me at all levels of the company.

Management took notice and promoted me to team leader within seven months. I received the second-fastest promotion to management in the company's history. The same boss who had hired me was now my peer.

With my new role came more responsibilities. I hired whom I wanted on my own team and looked for traits similar to my own: dependable, able to take rejection, understands time management, and can meet goals. I paid particular attention to weak personal behavior, like the reporter who couldn't meet her deadlines. I asked the same of them as I would have of myself: "Share with me a time when you didn't meet a goal and why." "How often did this happen?" "Tell me a situation when you ran into a problem and how you solved it."

Let's say you are just trying to get a job. Any job. Perhaps you just came to this country, or moved to the big city from the boondocks. You are entering the workforce for the first time. These are the questions you may be asked. "Tell us a little bit about yourself." "What would your former employer say are your strengths and weaknesses?" "Share with us your skills and educational background." "Tell us why you should be hired." Regardless of the types of questions, hiring managers want to know if you fall into the victim trap of "making excuses" for which they have zero tolerance. And, if you do, they'll toss your résumé in the trash.

Now that I was managing people, I also learned how to develop relationships with my employees, act as a mentor, and help sharpen their communication and business skills. I used a lot of what I learned from reporting about the importance of telling a story briefly and painting a vivid picture, especially since we were selling to clients over the phone and they didn't get to "test" the product. As a team leader, I was now responsible for making sure my team was performing. And, you bet during my quarterly performance reviews, my boss, the director of sales, cared about one thing—did I hit my goals? She didn't want to hear any excuses, especially since my numbers reflected on her performance as my boss, which then rolled up into the company's aggressive goals.

The company went from being privately held to a public corporation. It received numerous accolades, including being ranked as the 4th Fastest Growing Technology Company in North America by Deloitte and Touche. At that time, Google was ranked #1 with the same title.

Had I not executed on the expectations set before me, I would have been in the way of the company's ultimate goal—to make a profit for its investors. I was hired to perform.

Talent, Looks, and Brains Can Only Take You So Far

I think that's what some people forget, especially those with any of these attributes; the world doesn't revolve around them. There is no sort of entitlement in life or in America. The world will keep moving on whether they're ready to show up or not.

As an example, there was a sales account executive at the company where I was a team leader. She had one of the best pitches I've ever heard when it came to articulating the features and benefits of the products to our clients, and had the ability to close anyone. I believe her strong business and communication skills came naturally from watching her father who was a big-time executive.

Unfortunately, though, while she was solid at hitting her numbers, she thought her talent alone was enough for her to keep her job. But, her skills were soon overlooked when she showed up late to work or didn't show up at all. If she was at work, she became a distraction as she spent quite a bit of time socializing. While her numbers were impressive, she didn't carry the whole load. And her behavior caused morale problems and loss of productivity throughout the sales floor.

Sadly, this was a talented individual who also happened to be a good friend of mine. Regardless of how much coaching I gave her as a friend and as her boss regarding the expectations of the job, she didn't listen. She was given many chances, but eventually her poor behavior, another kind of excuse, caught up with her. She was let go.

This attitude followed her to her next job, too, where a friend recommended her to work at her company. Unfortunately, the same thing happened there as it did at her previous job. She was the same "employee," behaving poorly at a different company. She was fired again.

In the end, my friend really hurt herself as employers were afraid to take a chance on her despite her being a solid sales person. She hopped from one sales job to another. Because she had no steady income, she charged up an enormous credit card debt and had to file for bankruptcy.

Another friend of mine also had to hit rock bottom to realize his excuses were taking over his life. His house was foreclosed on, he racked up nearly $200,000 in debts, and lost his girlfriend and some good friends along the way. That was when he realized his excuses were costing him everything he had worked so hard to attain, and he finally looked at himself in the mirror and realized he had a gambling problem.

This is a guy whose family immigrated to America with the clothes on their back, but he didn't let that stop him. He was certainly on his way, chasing after the American Dream when he graduated from college, earned a respectable job in medical sales, and bought his own house. He rewarded his accomplishments with a little gambling here and there. But, it got out of hand and he ended up lying to his girlfriend, friends, and family about why he couldn't pay his bills. He started to borrow money from them despite earning a decent income himself, and people began to question his ethics. He lost their trust.

There's a happy ending to my friends' stories, as they both cleaned up their acts. It cost them lots of money and severed some relationships along the way, but they eventually learned their lessons: their excuses were costing them a better life. They took a good hard look at themselves and got professional help to correct their poor behavior. They deserved better, and so did their family and friends.

Just as our minds allow us to make excuses or justify our behavior, we can also step back and observe ourselves. It takes practice to condition our minds to catch these excuses before we fall into the trap of unconscious behavior. Think of this mental stance like you're exercising a muscle that hasn't been used for a while. When you begin to train that muscle, you may be sore the first day. But, that soreness eventually goes away. The muscle gets used to the training. It is the same thing when it comes to watching our behavior and not making excuses for it. It's always easier to be mentally lazy rather than finding solutions. But, if you want more out of life and want to get ahead, you've got to make a conscious choice to come up with a resolution when you're faced with a roadblock. Better yet, start thinking ahead of possible challenges you may come across that you could prevent or steer clear of from the start. Let's say you don't have enough money for transportation; you have to see what else in your expenses you can cut out. Does that mean moving in with someone to save money for rent or mortgage? Does that mean not buying cigarettes or alcohol? As long as you are willing to work hard and be disciplined, you can certainly free yourself of "excuses," and get on with your life.

Take Matters into Your Own Hands

As I shared with you in the preface, I was fired from my first job as a reporter. It was at that same station where I had rearranged my life all within seventy-two hours to make sure I showed up to work on time. I really wanted to make a good impression on my boss to show that I was someone who followed through with an agreement.

But, somewhere in the course of our working relationship, he had different plans for my future, which didn't include me as part of his team. He never questioned my strong work ethic, loyalty, or passion. He had concerns about my accent, my storytelling, and . . . After so many one-on-ones with him, I was just waiting for the shoe to drop.

Losing my job would certainly be a blow to the ego. But, how would I pay my rent? I knew I still had six months left on my lease. I was also real with myself when things started going downhill. I had financial responsibilities, and I had to think of a Plan B.

So, I started working my contacts to let them know I might be looking for another position in this market sometime soon.

I was right. The shoe did drop, and I was out of a job. But, since I anticipated being let go, I had interviewed at the number-one station, where I was hired just twenty-four hours after I was fired.

I was relieved that I could pay my rent and make my car payments. I didn't have to call my family and ask for help. I didn't want to involve them in my problems.

Most importantly, I was grateful for my new job. This was my chance to prove to the station that it had made the right hire and to prove to myself that I was destined to be a reporter.

I could've used my first boss as an excuse for not continuing to chase my dreams as a reporter. I didn't. I took matters into my own hands. So should *you*. Going after your dreams is not going to be easy. Only the people with mental fortitude will get what they want in life.

CHAPTER TWO

When Adversity Bites Your Butt

When you hear the word *adversity*, what comes to mind? Crisis? Challenges? Changes? I kind of had an idea what adversity meant when Mom told me that she just got her first job in America. After filling out dozens of applications noting her job history in the Philippines and only being rejected, Mom finally got a job as a housekeeper for a hotel near the airport.

"Maureen," she explained, "we all have to start somewhere. Let this be an important lesson to you. This isn't what I imagined as my job in America, but I need money to support us," Mom said.

At a tender age, I drew my own conclusions about adversity. It meant life wasn't giving Mom what she wanted right now. It meant Mom was going to do something she didn't really like doing: take a job out of her comfort zone. But, through Mom's example, I learned what adversity didn't mean: making an excuse for falling short of your goals now, being unhappy about your circumstances, or quitting on life and your future. I learned adversity can be handled with grace and with gumption. And, not all adversity is a bad thing. It builds character, which is one of the keys to success.

Be Grateful for What You Have

If you knew my mom, you knew she wasn't one to clean houses. In fact, in the Philippines, we had a maid who did the housework and a nanny to take care of me. Mom was a professional working woman. (Despite the humble living conditions, it's not uncommon in the Philippines to have a maid, as she or he was paid very little and the job likely included room and board.)

Her new role as a housekeeper was certainly a major downgrade for her, since she was college-educated and had worked in the communications field in Manila. She had been ahead of her time back home when she became a working single parent after my father's death. She worked an office job, which was rare for a woman of her generation.

And, now she was making beds and cleaning toilets for minimum wage. It was hard to see her in that job, knowing her potential, but she had no other options.

That was when I learned that sometimes you have to do something you don't really want to do in life, but your circumstances demand it. It's part of life, especially for immigrants or those without a stellar education. It's an adversity, but it doesn't have to be a death knell.

I knew Mom preferred an office job, but I also knew she didn't have the luxury of waiting, considering she had a daughter who depended on her. She needed money right away. Money provided shelter. Money paid for our food. I understood Mom's job meant she would earn money and meet her obligations, as they say.

Yet, as Mom put on her uniform, I never saw her mad at God or at others for being stuck with a low-paying, low-status job. She never let the job define who she was as a person or limit her possibilities. Instead, she kept telling me how grateful she was to be able to provide for us.

Mom has always been a grateful person. She focuses her energy on what she has and works for what she wants. Mom knew her pay wasn't much. But, she is a smart woman who knew the possibilities of advancement if she worked hard enough and proved herself to her boss and other managers in the company. She picked up extra shifts and worked holidays. When she got frustrated flipping over a mattress, Mom once again focused on what she had. "This job supports my family. It has excellent benefits," she'd say. And, that was all it took to keep the right attitude. That's how Mom had always been—always appreciative and never ungrateful for life's blessings.

Only Good Things Come from Being Positive

Because Mom was grateful, it was natural for her to have a positive attitude, and it showed in her work and her interaction with people. Her company took notice. After a year in housekeeping, the hotel promoted her to receptionist and eventually to program coordinator for the catering department. She worked hard for those promotions, and in the literal sense knew how to clean house—well. She even swept up an award as Employee of the Month.

I remembered my mom's life example and the lessons lived when I accepted my very first on-air job in Yakima. My friends and family congratulated me wholeheartedly, knowing how tough it was to break into the TV news business. I was grateful for the opportunity. But then reality sunk in as I was confronted with the unglamorous side of the business: lugging around a twenty-pound tripod in one hand and a camera in the other hand, and changing and doing makeup in a moving van. Because I was a newbie, my news director sent me each day all over the city to pick up the stories nobody else wanted. By the time I got back to the station, I had little time to get the video footages edited and write the stories that the anchors would read. The timid need not apply for this job.

When I'd get home, I'd often fall asleep in bed wearing my work clothes. Because I worked so hard, it would have been easy to focus on my humble salary and my demanding and ungrateful boss. But, I knew if I did that, in the end this attitude would sabotage me and I would only be hurting myself. Dwelling on the negative meant that I would pull energy away from being the best reporter I could be, which was my main goal.

In the news business, the people in the industry are trained to be critical of the story, the video, and the newscast. They're in the business of perfection. They have to be: any on-air miscue is glaring. I'm no different. I strive for excellence, too. For example, I'd go through a can of hairspray in a few weeks. I wanted my hair to look perfect for the camera where no strands would fly away. Even if it was breezy, which it often was in the Northwest, my hair stayed perfectly still.

So, it took a lot of mental strength and focus for me to keep a positive attitude every day. Trust me, there were days that were particularly tough to be "Pollyanna," especially when my boss yelled at the news team or me, mostly for things out of our control. We couldn't help it if the editing machine was jammed an hour prior to the newscast that day and we couldn't give our story our best effort. As a result, the video looked like it was slapped together, because it really was. There was no time to fix the edits. Otherwise, we risked not meeting the deadline. Let me tell you, the yelling was a whole lot louder for missed deadlines than for sloppy edits.

My news director's yelling and general approach proved to be a good example for me. I told myself that I would never manage a team using fear tactics. When I became a manager and my team wasn't producing the results I wanted, I never yelled at them. I found positive ways to get their "buy-in," whether it was a pep talk, rolling up my sleeves and pitching in myself, or asking them point-blank, "Team, we're not performing well. What can we do?" I learned like many managers before me that you get better results with a carrot than a stick.

Life's Adversities Are Just Temporary Hiccups

You may find yourself in a job—or work for a boss—you don't like. Personal relationships may seem unmanageable, or the company may be heading in a different direction than you'd prefer and you find yourself struggling to find anything "positive" in your situation. I've been there, so will you, and even the best of us who've done our research face adversity. I remember a keynote speech from an entrepreneur who learned success the hard way.

Ben Huh's first startup company wasn't a winner. Today, he's the CEO and owner of Cheezburger, one of the largest online humor publishers in the world.

As an immigrant to this country from Korea, Ben's entrepreneurial spirit and positive attitude gave him the confidence to start his own web analytics software company, Raydium, in 2000. "It didn't last very long, only eighteen months. When the dot-com bubble burst, we couldn't raise enough money to keep afloat. So my first venture as an entrepreneur was very brief and very brutal."

Despite surrounding himself with business-savvy entrepreneurs and taking their advice, Ben still made costly mistakes. Lots of them.

"People told me, 'You'll spend too much time raising money and not enough time with your product. You won't spend enough time actually getting customers to buy your product.' They told me all the mistakes I'd make and I said, 'No, I 'm not going to make those mistakes.' And, I went ahead and made them anyway."

Ben found himself $40,000 in debt. He put a lot of the company's expenses on his personal credit card. "So, when the company folded, I had a lot of debt obligations to pay off in addition to my student loans." With his options limited, Ben put his ego aside and got a J-O-B with one condition. "I'm going to get a job with people who are successful entrepreneurs."

He accepted a position as general manager of his friend's startup Internet radio company. Ben's friend was a seasoned entrepreneur. "I was the number two guy there, and was getting paid $8.50 an hour. Basically, I really needed to learn how to be an entrepreneur while keeping a salaried job."

The entrepreneurship lessons Ben learned from his first start-up bust remained fresh in his mind. With more debt than savings, Ben lived in a four-bedroom apartment with roommates to make ends meet. The costly mistake he made as a first-time CEO taught him to be frugal, to be sustainable, or else his resources would be depleted; and most of all, he told himself: don't ignore good advice. "Learn from other people's mistakes."

For the next six years, Ben was disciplined with his finances and watched the mistakes others around him made. When he received a second chance to be CEO of his own company in 2007, he was debt-free and had the training to make *I Can Has Cheezburger* one of the largest social networking blogs in the world. With every mistake he made or saw others make, he promised himself he wouldn't repeat them again with this new venture. "Be lean and mean. Build something that users value before investing more money. Prove before you buy. But most important, I wanted to slay all the sacred cows that made me assume businesses had to be a certain way. This time around, I was going to listen, but find my own way to success."

Today, Ben runs more than sixty humor websites including I Can Has Cheezburger?, FAIL Blog, Know Your Meme, Memebase, and The Daily What.

Cheezburger counts a passionate fan base of twenty-four million people who view five hundred million pages per month.

Just like Ben, remember that your situation is temporary. It's not forever, permanent, or a life-sentence. It's only endless if you make it that way with a bad attitude.

I remember managing a team member who still couldn't get over a divorce that happened five years earlier. She often brought her emotional baggage with her to work, and it prevented her from reaching her earning potential. While I had empathy for her and her situation—my fiancé and I broke up around the same time—I never let my personal life get in the way of doing my job. There were days I didn't know which person she would be bringing to work that day—the employee who was trapped in the past and unable to focus, or the bright woman who was ready to close business. With sales, if you don't have a good attitude, it usually carries into your interaction with people and prevents you from bringing your A-game.

I had another team member who also had a chip on his shoulder. When the company made decisions that didn't help his bottom line, he'd voice his disappointment to everyone for weeks on end. When he applied to be a sales manager, his numbers were good enough to get him the promotion, but the boss also considered his attitude and whether he'd be able to think company first, his bottom line second. As a result, he was passed up on a promotion every time that a manager position became open. Had this employee managed his frustration privately or with his superiors behind closed doors, I'm certain that he would've been promoted.

Both of these employees were trapped by their past and couldn't bring the full force of their personalities and talents to the table day in and day out. My advice to them and to you is just drop it, or you'll drop the ball for yourself and those who depend on you.

Set Goals that Keep You on Track

When I was living in my studio apartment working my first job, away from family and friends and pursuing my dream to be a TV reporter, I would often look at my written-down goals. And when I did, my current situation would make more sense. Goals reminded me I was on the right path, not stuck in a ditch. Goals gave me a sense of control and certainty. I CHOSE to take a job away from my family and friends because I was chasing my dream to be a reporter. I CHOSE to live in a humble studio apartment because it was all I needed at that time. I CHOSE to live in small-town Yakima because it was where I got my first big break. I CHOSE to be in a good mood. When faced with adversity like losing my job, I just brushed aside the anxiety and quickly found a better job. I said, "Not today" to my fears. Because I had goals and a plan telling me with a smile, "Don't listen to adversity," I stayed on track with my dreams intact.

I learned to look at my goals on a regular basis, which allowed me to have better time management. They boosted my confidence and self-esteem and kept me on track.

So, if it appears life isn't giving you want you want or planned, look at your situation again. Can you learn anything that you can apply to your set of goals? Is what's happening in your life making you humble, determined, or compassionate? I believe there's something to be learned in any situation.

I also recommend that when you create goals, you make them measurable and realistic. "I want to be a TV reporter." (Okay.) But, is this a measurable goal? Is it specific? No, as it doesn't answer the following questions: When is this going to take place? Where is my ideal reporting situation? How am I going to get there? Here's a better way to write down this particular goal:

"I want to be a television reporter in Seattle within five years. I am going to get there by embracing all my news assignments, doing them well and by the deadlines, and by asking questions of anybody who can teach me something. This way I will eventually be chosen as the top story reporter where I am sent out on breaking news and stories that get me at the top of the hour. As a result, this will help me hone my writing and reporting skills to make a résumé tape that will allow me to move up in markets and eventually back to Seattle."

Now, that's a measurable, specific goal with a clear plan! Each year at each job, my storytelling improved and I was often the top story reporter. Each year, I sent out my résumé tape. Each year, I climbed markets and by my fifth year as a reporter, I was *finally* reporting in my own backyard—Seattle.

But, in the midst of my journey to Seattle, I had days that seemed like I was just running on a treadmill and not going anywhere; there were setbacks and blown assignments. *Wait a minute. Aren't I doing my dream job of reporting?* That was when I reminded myself that I was in complete control of my destiny and that accepting adversity was all part of my plan to get to my big goal. So, when I hopped from Yakima, Washington, to Savannah, Georgia, to Flint, Michigan, or to cities that still weren't my first-market choice, I told myself: ALL of this was part of the *big picture* of where my goals were taking me.

When I had switched careers from being an on-air reporter to sales, my goal then was to make money. At the time I had a huge pile of debts from student loans, credit cards, car payments, and bills. I didn't question myself or ask "what if" about my decision to leave the news business because, in the end, it was *my* choice.

I was very good at sales and was soon able to wipe out my debts. By exceeding my goals and my sales quotas, the company rewarded me with a promotion within a year.

On the other hand, when the real estate market went bust in 2007, the company started to downsize and eliminated several team leaders, including me. When I got the news that my position had been eliminated, I accepted the news with grace and professionalism. As it turned out, the company didn't want to lose me and offered me a position as an individual sales contributor.

Now, I could've declined that offer and taken the severance package, and had time to look for another job. But, that would have meant walking away from my stock options. Leaving the company altogether would hurt *my* big picture, which was to earn a certain income on a certain schedule. There was money on the table, or a bird in hand, and I accepted my new role with my goals intact.

But then your big picture can get shrunk sometimes by the ups and downs of your career, and that's when you learn one of life's big lessons:

Fail to Succeed

I have shared with you what happened at my first on-air news job. But when it came to my third job, this time as a weekend anchor, reporter, and producer in Savannah, Georgia, I figured I was well on my way.

During my time in Savannah, I interviewed some high-profile celebrities, like Academy Award-winning director, actor, and producer Sydney Pollack, as well as Paula Deen—today's face for Southern food and living—before she became a media mogul, and many others.

Unfortunately, after one year, I was laid off from this job even though the weekend show had better ratings than the weekday shows. I didn't see this coming. I was quickly learning that this was part of the business and found myself moving back to Seattle. This was not the way I imagined my success story. I really didn't want to go back to Seattle *unless* I had a high-profile reporting job. Quite honestly, I felt like I had failed. Once again, adversity somehow stole my thunder.

But, then I reminded myself that this is where I was after my first reporting job. And, like then, I had *control* of my next move. It was up to me to pick myself up off the floor after a surprise punch and get up and get going.

I wouldn't say my experience in Savannah was a total failure. My storytelling improved. My grasp of what is "news" got better. My confidence to go to the scene of a breaking news story and tell the story as it unfolded turned a corner. Overall, I was a better reporter.

But, how was I better when I was, once again, without a job? I learned that for every failure, I developed new insight in life that would lead to success: I had adapted to a new environment and different kinds of people, added needed skills, learned to cope without close friends and family, and came away with a better audition reel.

So, if you find yourself in America or a big city for the first time and aren't seeing overnight success, take a look at my work history. Life didn't give me anything. It made me earn everything. I was now three years into television reporting, and I certainly was better at it, but I was again without a job. Twenty-four hours after being laid off, I didn't receive a phone call with the message "You're hired." In fact, weeks went by and no phone call, which then turned into months. I started to get worried. Was my career over before it really had gotten started?

During this unexpected change in my life, I moved into an apartment near Seattle and did a contract job as a copywriter for Costco's online business unit to pay my bills. As you well know, my student loans, car payment, credit card companies, and landlords didn't care that I got laid off. In the interim, I had to do a job for which I had no passion, but in a company I did respect.

That's when I could hear Mom's voice, "Be grateful for what you have." As I looked around at a life that I didn't imagine for myself, I could be grateful that my contract job paid the bills and didn't put my finances in jeopardy. While I wasn't writing and chasing down news stories, I got to develop new skills—online content. I was grateful that I got to spend more time with my fiancé. I was also grateful that from my mother I'd learned that I had the resilience to not let anyone or my situation pull me away from my dreams.

At night and on the weekends, I kept submitting audition tapes and writing letters to news directors. I also hired an agent to get me leads for possible jobs. I was working every angle imaginable. And, as my contract job at Costco was about to expire, I would like to tell you I was fearless. Wrong! Fear started to creep in as I asked myself where I would get my next paycheck. Thank goodness, someone up there or out there heard me. I finally got a phone call.

"Maureen . . ." said my talent agent, who always seemed pressed for time. "The NBC affiliate in mid-Michigan got your audition tape and likes it."

After a four-month drought, I finally felt a raindrop. And unlike other TV job interviews, this station flew me in for an interview so I could see the city and meet with the news team. I felt absolutely special being "wined and dined."

Flint isn't exactly a world-famous tourist delight like Savannah. It was a city right out of a 1930s Depression-era newsreel. Flint was largely dependent on the automotive industry to fuel its economy. When factories closed shop for cheaper labor overseas, tens of thousands of people lost jobs. And, you could see the effects: dilapidated buildings, burned-down houses, and graffiti all over public buildings. Sounds like paradise, huh?

When the station offered me a job, did I take it? Yes. I liked the people; in fact, they were a lot like me: tough, nose to the grindstone, pulling flowers out of trash bins. I knew this experience would help further define me as a reporter because I would be telling harder news stories and seeing the best in these dire situations.

When I moved into my biggest apartment to date, I couldn't help but celebrate inside. I had come a long way. I wouldn't be where I was if I had not failed. Failure allowed me to embrace adversity every time it came my way. Failure built character in me. Failure showed me resilience. And it put me where my perpetual optimism could do the best: a failed community looking for hope. I could see it in them because I could see it first in myself.

Nobody is a fan of adversity, but I recommend you learn to appreciate its tests and challenges, because they're the stepladder to success.

You can imagine the adversity a minority woman and immigrant had to face in the military to become the first woman to head the

White House Medical Unit. Through mutual business contacts and friends, Dr. Connie Mariano became my mentor. In situations when adversity came knocking at her door, Dr. Mariano didn't get discouraged. It gave her a reason to encourage others to change their behaviors. "Climbing the ladder meant educating people that their stereotypes and assumptions were wrong. When people look at us diminutive, petite, Asian women, they assume we are quiet, meek, and subservient—the stereotypical servant women of the Orient. That is the biggest challenge Asian Pacific women face. And, if we are attractive, which most Asian women are, they assume we are not smart enough or that we got our jobs because of our good looks. Our attractiveness is held against us. So for jobs requiring 'American' behavior—bold, assertive, tough, macho—Asian American women have to prove that we are intelligent, strong, and assertive and can compete in the American workplace."

With that attitude, Dr. Mariano shattered the "glass ceiling" or "bamboo ceiling," by being the first Filipino American in US history to become a navy rear admiral. Given her background, this was quite an accomplishment: being the immigrant daughter of a Filipino Navy steward. "It was a major achievement not only to become an officer, but to rise to the rank of admiral. I grew up the daughter of a steward, entering through the kitchen door to visit my father in the homes of admirals where we served them Sunday dinner. As an admiral, I didn't have to enter 'through the kitchen door' anymore." She never once let adversity get in her way.

Learn How to Embrace Adversity

One way or another you may find yourself facing these questions: "Did you lose a job?" "Get passed up on a promotion?" "Move to a new city?"

Now, ask yourself these questions: "Why did you fear the adversity?" "How did you handle that adversity?" "How would you coach yourself when adversity is inevitable?"

I've learned over time that accepting changes takes practice. It is something for which you need to condition and train your mind. If you find yourself saying, "I don't like change. Period. That's just how I am," you are not alone. Those are the very same words I also used, but like me, you will learn either to roll with the punches or to get stuck—permanently. Remember that employee who still talked about her divorce as though it had happened yesterday? It cost her not only her happiness, but achieving her income goal.

If I hadn't accepted adversity, I would never have had the courage to get out of my comfort zone. It would have been way too easy for me when I moved back to Seattle to just stay there. After all, I was living in my city with family, friends, and my fiancé. Personally, it was a good move. Professionally, I never wanted to ask myself, "What if I didn't give up?" "What if I just stuck with my five-year goal? Could I have made it to Seattle as a TV reporter?"

If you are really not there yet with adversity, that's okay. Just keep the transformations in your life small. With time, you'll be able to handle real adversity when it comes knocking at your door. I would not have had the courage to move to Flint, Michigan, for a job right out of college. Come on. It's a tough city. I had to build my tolerance for adversity.

A study shows that people who focused on at least three good things that were happening in their lives and wrote them down every day for six straight weeks had more optimism, fewer physical ailments, and better sleep. I didn't start journaling my gratitude until much later in life. I wish I had done it sooner. So, what I did was write down three things that I was grateful for in my life. It would be something as simple as: "I'm grateful for my cappuccino in the morning." "I'm grateful that my friend phoned me." "I'm grateful for . . ." Now, when you write down three things that you are grateful for each day, try to make them different. Try journaling right before you go to bed, and you'll be able to "focus" on the good things going on in your life. After journaling what you are grateful for, you will realize there are a lot of positive things happening in your life and reasons for you to smile even though you're in the midst of adversity. You'll be able to say "Bring it on!"

CHAPTER THREE

The Value of Money

I learned the value of money from my adoptive father. In his own unique way and just by being himself, Dad showed me the importance of money and how to be frugal. Growing up, I watched him always being fiscally responsible, saving a buck here and there. As soon as he'd leave a room, he'd immediately turn off the lights. He'd brush his teeth without the water running. If the house was cold, he'd put on more clothes and not turn the heat up. Any leftovers would not go to waste as he made another meal from them.

I remember him lecturing me as a child. "Everything costs money; you know . . . lights, food, water, gas. None of it is free," he told me after I left the lights on in the kitchen. With his eyebrow raised and with a stern look, he continued, "Someone's paying for these things." I knew that he was talking about himself.

Dad's mom lived through the Great Depression. So, she saw some tough times and passed her frugal ways on to her son. But, I was just six years old, so I just saw Dad as a penny pincher. Cheap. I wouldn't really appreciate his thriftiness until I moved into my own apartment and started to pay my own bills. Then I understood why Dad wasn't wasteful. I finally gained an appreciation of why he was so manic about us turning up the heat. When I opened my first gas bill, I realized that I had to adopt Dad's attitude.

Be Cheap or Go Broke

Those first few months on my own, as you will learn when you leave the nest or get your first place in America, I quickly discovered the difference between my wants and real needs.

I wanted my MTV. I needed food.

I wanted to go to the movies. I needed to pay my electric bill.

I wanted to get my eyebrows professionally waxed. I needed to do it myself, or NOT. (There were some things I just couldn't skimp on. I was an on-air TV reporter and funny-looking eyebrows weren't acceptable.)

For the most part, I was surprisingly good at compartmentalizing my wants versus needs.

Had I not adopted Dad's frugality, my dream of being a TV reporter would've ended sooner, and I would've been forced to trade the microphone for a computer screen in a higher paying desk job. At that time, I wasn't exactly taking home Katie Couric's paycheck. In case you're just off the boat or never watched television, she makes a ton of money interviewing high-profile people living their dreams.

Let's face it. We all have dreams. It's what brought my mother to America and maybe you or your parents, or why you left the farm for the big city. That brings me to my next insight:

Will That Be Plastic or Paper or Cash?

As you can surmise, I'm not talking about your grocery bags. (If I were, I'd insist on cloth.) I'm talking about forms of payment.

A family friend from the Philippines was so impatient about achieving her American Dream that she paid for it with loans and on credit cards. Days after getting her green card, Wendy got a job as a dietician's aide working for a senior citizen community. I admired her tenacity for being a go-getter and finding a job quickly. She had the presentation skills to sell herself, and she knew how to bring her A-game to the interview.

But, when it came to managing her finances, she got an "F." She had absolutely no concept of the value of money, and thus she didn't respect it and spent it too freely.

I got to witness Wendy's lack of financial skills when I accompanied her to an auto dealership to buy a car for her job.

It was apparent our family friend had been there a few times.

"Hi Wendy. Nice to see you again," said salesperson 1.

"Welcome back, Wendy," said salesperson 2.

"Hi, guys," Wendy said, batting her eyelashes.

It was clear that Wendy wasn't just window-shopping that day for a car. She had her mind set on a Ford Explorer, which was considered a luxury vehicle in the Philippines, and something Wendy had been wanting for years.

She found a white Explorer and was mesmerized. "I'll take it," she said, and looked like a giddy sixteen-year-old.

"Are you sure?" I said in shock. I did the math, and it didn't end up in Wendy's favor. Many financial experts say that people should set aside six to eight months of living expenses in case of an emergency. The SUV's price tag was equivalent to her entire year's salary. I was convinced that she'd struggle to keep up the payments along with her other bills.

"Are you sure?" I said again, hoping she would reconsider. "Have you done the math? What about your rent, groceries, and utility bills? How will you manage this payment in addition to everything else?"

As I stared into her glazed eyes, I knew my words weren't sinking in. It was as if I were speaking in a foreign language. *Had she thought about how her entire paycheck would go toward her payment? What would she live on?* I asked myself. I could just see a disaster in the making, and I was completely powerless to stop it. I was in my early twenties back then, and Wendy was a full-fledged adult, close to her mid-thirties. There was no way she was going to take advice from someone younger, yet I felt like I was the parent. I resigned myself—the only way Wendy could ever learn the value of money was by totally mismanaging it, as in this case.

Because she was the youngest of ten children, Wendy had been given everything. She just never understood the consequences of her actions because there was always someone bailing her out, either her parents or older siblings.

Had she been surrounded with people who coached her about the value of money, I don't think Wendy would have even considered making such a huge financial investment, like buying a car, when the math just didn't add up.

Jesse Tam, who is in the banking industry and has two grown sons who sit on the Ascend board with me, told me he wanted to raise his children to be independent. Today, they are both successful young adults in leadership roles. Jesse said that he wanted to take a different approach to raising his sons than what his own father had done. Jesse wanted a healthy dialogue with his children regarding the decisions they made by treating them like adults when they were young. This was quite opposite from the traditional way his father raised him by being the parental supreme power and treating Jesse as a child with no opinion. There was very little communication between the two of them.

Jesse said lessons on how his children could start to think for themselves and understand the consequences began with normal activities like buying them toys.

"I would ask my son, 'This is your choice?'"

"And he would say, 'Yes Dad. I want it. I want it. I want it.'"

"I said, 'Okay if you want it. What is your contribution?'"

"He would say, 'Dad, this is a ten-dollar toy. If I use all my savings in my little piggy bank, I only come up with five dollars.'"

"I would then say, 'Okay. As your father, I can help you out and contribute five for your five, so it comes to ten dollars to buy the toy. Remember, this is your choice. And, this is your decision, and I hope you will like it.'"

According to Jesse, that approached worked well with his children, and if something happened with a toy, like it broke, which this one did a week later, he would put the consequence back on his children. And his son couldn't blame him. "What did you learn?" Jesse asked his boy.

"He said, 'Well, I spent everything I had on a toy that lasted one week. From now on, I have to be more careful with my money.'"

Jesse added that this lesson was no longer about the toy, but the choices his sons made and the consequences of their decisions. Jesse said, "It turned out to be the best education they ever got. Much more than school ever taught them. It's about how to responsibly, take control of their lives, and continue to exercise that."

Those lessons throughout his children's lives built a foundation for clear communication with them that only grew stronger as adults. Oftentimes, he turns to them for advice. "They have grown up to become men, rather than always my little boys; I couldn't be their father forever. Someday I will not be around. I always wanted them to make their own decisions, to search for their own answers. I wanted them to learn how to think and take a leadership role in life."

It's unfortunate that Wendy never got those early lessons in life about choices and consequences.

As I sat next to her, all I could say was, "Okay," and flash a fake smile as my stomach churned.

I watched Wendy sign the dotted line and become an owner of a new, white, four-door Ford Explorer.

Well, nearly a decade later, Wendy was able to pay off her SUV. But, she wasn't able to pay off her credit cards, which was how she fueled her American Dream with new TVs, clothes, and a trip back to the Philippines. She paid for them with loans and credit cards, since her humble salary couldn't come close to paying for them in cash.

Wendy worked overtime and holidays, and she earned the most money she'd ever made in America, but she was always in the red. She was already living with her daughter in a two-bedroom apartment with another family to save money on rent, yet Wendy was still short on cash. She turned to her family and friends (and even me) to borrow cash.

So why did a woman who grew up in humble circumstances try to buy her way into the American Dream all at once, rather than earning it step by step? Who gave her the idea that she didn't have to live on her income? Where is the disconnect? It can only be one thing . . .

Human ATM Machines Eventually Run Dry

Wendy's sister Lisa was the first in her family to come to America. She didn't have anyone sending her money from abroad. She was the one who had to pave the way for others, unlike her sister who got accustomed to receiving a monthly check from Lisa or their parents. So Wendy came to think of America as a place where money grew on trees.

Before coming to the States, when Wendy was living in the Philippines and had financial woes there, she'd write to her sister begging for her help. Lisa never hesitated and would send money overseas to her sister. Being the older sister, Lisa thought she was helping Wendy. This went on for years. Lisa was unknowingly becoming an enabler. Though her intentions were good, in reality, she was inhibiting her sister from being able to stand on her own two feet and figuring out ways to get out of the messes she created for herself. So, when Wendy came to America (again, with Lisa's help) and had the same money troubles, she again relied on her sister Lisa or their parents to bail her out.

At forty, Wendy's financial skills didn't get any better, and she was still spending way more money than she was making. After years of charging everything to her credit card, she was only paying the interest and never the principal.

Wendy's money woes also strained her relationship with her family, including Lisa, as they got tired of her always asking for money. Finally Lisa stopped contributing to the problem by no longer being her sister's human ATM machine. After watching her sister's money troubles only get worse, Lisa realized that she was equally to blame for Wendy's financial problems.

Well, the tough love started to work, as Wendy had no other option but to juggle two jobs to make ends meet. Unfortunately, this taxed her relationship with her daughter as she was always working and didn't spend enough time with her during those critical formative years of a child's life.

Is Wendy debt-free today? No, but she's thinking twice before making any big purchases. With her credit cards maxed out, Wendy came to the realization that no one was there to rescue her the next time she found herself so pinched for cash that she couldn't buy groceries or gas for the car.

If Your Family Doesn't Give You Tough Love, Life Will

Here's a similar story about a family who thought they were helping a loved one by always being there for him. This friend, Mike, had parents who showed him affection through gifts. His parents are immigrants to this country from Korea and wanted the best for their son. Before he turned eighteen, his parents bought him a two-thousand-dollar watch. Why?

A) Did he get good grades?
B) Was he accepted into college?
C) Did he find a cure for cancer?
D) None of the above.

The answer is D. His parents bought him the watch simply because he was their *only* son. As he got older, the gifts got bigger. For his twenty-first birthday, they bought him a brand new car. They even gave him an allowance in his early twenties. Now, his parents weren't rich, or even well off. He came from a middle-income family.

Unfortunately, Mike's parents were not teaching their son the value of money. The cash his parents gave him was spent on friends or gambling. Like Wendy, he had no clue about managing his finances. He'd shop 'til he dropped and charged the items or clothes as if he had unlimited funds and his parents' allowance would continue for a lifetime.

But, when his parents' business took a turn for the worse, the gravy train stopped for their son. It was the best thing that could've happened to this friend. He had no choice but to rely on his job for his only source of income as his parents had no extra money for his "allowance." Their son struggled to stay at a job because he hadn't developed the skills to "tough it out." He was used to being the "king" at his house and had a tough time being a "subordinate" at work. So, he'd quit job after job. He didn't realize that companies typically don't care about your personal history; they just want you to perform your duties. And, he didn't get that *all* jobs came with their own set of problems. Things were not always going to go his way. He had a tough time grasping that concept, and he'd resign without having another job lined up. Being jobless only added to Mike's money woes.

I sat on the board of another nonprofit organization, the *International Examiner* (*IE*). The *IE* caters to Pan Asian American stories. Andy Yip is the president of the board (at the time of this interview). He is also the founder and owner of his own financial investment company called Raymond James. Most of Andy's clients are Asians.

Andy shared with me that saving money is natural for his immigrant clients, unlike for those who have lived in America for quite a while. During these tough economic times, Andy found them taking out loans or finding ways to pull out their investment money, which resulted in paying penalty fees. He noticed that this group of clients hadn't saved enough money for the rainy days.

Because immigrants or first-generation Americans have spent years being fiscally responsible, and in some cases missing out on their childhood, Andy says they tend to live vicariously through their children, making up for lost years. The conversation with their child might go something like this, "We came here to have a better lifestyle. Now we have a good paycheck. So, why don't you just enjoy your youth first? There will come a time later when you will make money."

This is quite the opposite of the immigrant mentality, which is work hard now and work hard later. It's not the same as the saying, "work hard now and play later."

Andy goes on, "So in a sense, they've gone from the extreme self-restriction of, 'I want to save every penny' to 'that's *my* job to save every penny. But for my kids, I want them to have the best lifestyle. I want them to go on a vacation first. I want to give them a down payment for their house. I want to be able to provide them with as much as possible, and then let them take on the real world.'"

Sadly, Andy says that the second generation becomes spoiled. The children suffer eventually because they haven't developed money management skills as adults. As in Wendy and Mike's cases, they think the money will never run out.

Even the Wealthy Have to Live Within Their Means

You saw the calamity that ensued when Wendy and Mike lived life with unlimited credit cards and nothing to back them up. They lost control of their lives. That's why it's important to live within your means. You saw how all the spending eventually caught up with Wendy as she was forced to work two jobs, which cost her personal time with her daughter. For Mike, it put him in such financial difficulties that he's still living with his parents as an adult.

Neither Wendy nor Mike came from families with large W2s. However, another executive came under the same spell of "overspending," which caused a wedge in her marriage. She said, "Rather than go into details, let's just say . . . becoming a millionaire when you're in your late twenties is dangerous. We spent too much and got too caught up in the race to 'get more.' Money can be a challenge in a relationship, not just a blessing."

There's a happy ending to this executive's story. For the next four years, she worked harder than she ever had, logging at least a hundred thousand air miles in those years and working eighty hours a week.

She eventually dug herself out of a financial grave after selling several companies by 2010 and became a millionaire once again. She said, "I had been a millionaire before. I knew how to do it again. It is pretty simple: take educated risks, be willing to make the sacrifices, and work your butt off. So many people think you can just get there without sacrifice and a ton of work. Very few of them can."

So what is the lesson behind her story?

Work Hard, Play Later

You may not have the "moxie" to build a multimillion-dollar company like that executive, but do you have the desire to work as hard as she did for what you want? She worked eighty hours a week to dig herself out of a financial grave. She had no choice but to put her head down and do the work.

I once found myself in a similar situation. I had lived on credit cards to keep my dream of being a reporter alive, but I came to a crossroad where I had to decide: do I stay in this high-status, low-paying job unable to pay student loans, car payments, and credit card bills? Or, do I take an opportunity presented to me and work in sales, knowing this company is going to go public? As you read in the previous chapter, I made a practical and realistic move versus an emotional decision. While I loved reporting, I also had financial responsibilities that weren't going away. Like my friend, I also put my head down and cranked it out. It wasn't as if someone was going to give me the winning lottery ticket. (But, I did get a chance at winning a million dollars on a game show, which I will talk about later.)

So, while I focused on replenishing my bank account, I made some changes in my living situation so I could live within my means. I moved into a studio apartment that was even smaller than the unit I had lived in in Yakima. This tiny studio only had room for my mattress and a dining table, which I had kept with me since my first apartment. My living situation was modest, but again, it was my choice, as I wanted to be financially sound.

For seven months, I lived in that studio and cut down on my expenses. I reintroduced my "wants" versus "needs" list with *every* buying decision. I had no gym membership and instead ran in the park. I didn't have Internet connection and checked my e-mails at work. And, I wouldn't allow myself to go shopping for clothes unless absolutely necessary.

When I went out with coworkers for happy hour, I skipped the alcohol. I'm not a big drinker to begin with, but I do like my Mojitos.

Back then, a juice would suffice. It took discipline and mental fortitude to get my finances to where I wanted them. Trust me, it wasn't easy. I was constantly being lured to stray from my financial goals.

"Maureen, do you want to go to the movies with us?"

"Maureen, how does your schedule look for going to this birthday party?"

"Maureen, you need more fun in your life."

One year after making a vow to address my financial woes, I was able to pay off *all* my debt. And, because I was able to live within my means, I replenished my bank account and could afford to throw myself a memorable thirtieth birthday party. The party was a gift to me. No one contributed to the bill; it was all me.

Too often, people think there's a way out of working hard. They try their luck at gambling, cut corners, or try other get-rich-quick schemes to achieve their goals. Don't be fooled by "chances." In the end, you'll just be disappointed, and your family and friends will pay the price, if they haven't already disowned you.

So Who Wants to Be an Off-the-Boat Millionaire?

This reminds me of a time where I had an opportunity at winning ten million dollars. CBS contacted me to be a contestant on *Power of Ten,* hosted by Drew Carey. I was part of TV history as the first contestant on the show—*and* just minutes away from a chance to win ten million dollars. It was the highest jackpot of any game show at that time. Drew was also making history as the host of two game shows, *Power of 10* and *The Price Is Right,* the longest-running daytime game show.

"So you ran four marathons?" Drew asked me.

"I did," I said. I was grinning ear to ear.

"Me, too," Drew said. The crowd chuckled.

After our small talk, it was on to the game.

Jamie, the other contestant, and I had to first go through an elimination round. The first person to guess three questions right went on to compete for the ten-million-dollar cash prize.

Drew said, "First question: What percentage of Americans says they have a better relationship with their parents as an adult than they did as a child?"

That would be me, I thought. But then I started thinking of all the children who let their parents live in nursing homes. I said to myself, *I'm going conservative with my answer.* I dialed to 56 percent.

Jamie guessed 74 percent.

We both watched as what looked like a thermometer on a screen flew past my guess on to Jamie's answer, and stopped at 89 percent. Jamie smiled and I said, "Good job."

The audience applauded.

Jamie was closest to the correct answer, and I got the first strike. Jamie just needed to accurately guess two more answers to kill my dream of being a millionaire. Drew said, "Question two: What percentage of Americans has spent more than a hundred dollars on a pair of jeans?"

That's me, I thought. *It's so hard to find a double zero pair of jeans, and when I do, they're usually more than a hundred dollars.*

"I always spend more than a hundred dollars on a pair of jeans as I have to use more material," Drew said.

The crowd laughed.

I locked it in—that was the catch phrase on the show—at 43 percent. Jamie put his down at 19 percent.

"You must know a lot of poor college kids," Drew said. The audience chuckled at Drew's joke. "Maureen is in marketing and must know a lot of people with money. She put down 43 percent. Let's see what America said."

The thermometer tricked me by moving up then going back down. Way down. Down. Down. And stopped at 10 percent.

I was surprised. Drew was too. "Wow! Hello Walmart! That's all I've got to say." The crowd roared.

Drew then asked the third and final question, which I again lost.

I was out. This could've been my *Slumdog Millionaire* story, or more accurately, an *Off-the-Boat Millionaire,* but it wasn't "written that way for me."

I shook Drew's hands and said "Good job" to Jamie.

He did a good job, had a real pulse on America. He didn't win the ten-million-dollar prize, but he didn't do badly either. He walked away a million dollars richer.

I saw my retirement money vanish before my eyes. This was my ticket, I thought, to not have to work forever. I realized then that I was going to have to earn my retirement money the old-fashion away—by keeping my day job and setting a certain amount aside each paycheck.

Pay Yourself First, Invest in Your Future

While I have had a lot of "day jobs," I continued to live within my means. Even when my salary fluctuated like the recent stock market yo-yo, I learned to readjust my spending and reintroduce a "budget" back into my life. I also made sure I set aside some money toward my future.

So should you, unless you plan to work forever. Don't get caught up in Wendy or Mike's world or lose absolutely everything by the time you turn forty or have to start all over like the executive.

So, you may be wondering, just how much money will you need for your retirement? I ask you: Just how big is your American Dream? I've heard of people who save between 5 percent and up to 10 percent of their salary and deposit it into their savings or retirement fund. Well . . . start saving and investing right now. You've got some work to do.

CHAPTER FOUR

Getting a Job, Keeping a Job, or Switching Jobs

Now that you're in America, or out of school, or in the big city, you've got to get a job, or two or three. Seriously. You have bills to pay, loans to pay off, and you have to maintain yourself. There is no such thing as a free lunch. This is especially true if you have people depending on you. Do you have children? A wife? A husband? Elderly parents here or back home?

Who You Know

When it comes to looking for a job, reach out to your friends and family and share with them that you are in the market to work. In this day and age, getting a job is all about who you know. When I had relatives who arrived from the Philippines, they got their respective jobs when family members made introductions for them to their employers. If they hadn't reached out to their sphere of friends and relatives, their job applications would have been lost in the pile of job seekers. This was a time when unemployment was in the double digits.

Let me be clear: my relatives had good work experience, having worked for the Philippine Embassy and having had their own businesses. Despite their solid résumés, their curricula vitae would have sat unattended. Potential employers don't have time to sort through to find the good ones. In most cases, hiring managers rely on their current employees' recommendations or their own network to find applicants. That's always been the case at my jobs. In fact, companies give bonuses for employee referrals because they know people like working with their friends.

Let me introduce you to another Maureen, Maureen Ezekwugo, or Maureen E. She was my boss at the first and second online start-up company I worked at. She got her job thanks to one of her former employees making an introduction to the hiring managers. Maureen E.

certainly had a solid résumé. She had previously worked at an online company managing more than one hundred sales people and seven sales teams. However, it was the introduction from a former employee that put her résumé at the top of the stack and also carried more weight in the job interview. Maureen E. wasn't just a number to them.

When Maureen E. was hired on at RealSelf.com—a website that educates consumers on whether elective surgery is right for them—she reached out to me first to fill a position that helped board-certified doctors navigate our site and coach them about being proactive about their online reputation.

At that time, I was working for an online marketing company and was offered a sales manager position. The company was growing fast. I wasn't really looking to switch from one company to another. But I knew Maureen E. was a powerhouse. So, I couldn't pass on an opportunity to work for her and be RealSelf's first senior doctor community advisor, a role where I helped pioneer an entirely new line of business for the company.

It was a good fit for me. Better fit for her. Like any good manager, Maureen E. knows that if she picks good employees, they'll make life easier and better for her. Choose unqualified workers, or those who are unaccountable, have bad attitudes, etc., and they'll drain your energy. Who you work with has a big impact on your daily life because you spend more time with your workmates than friends and family.

If Your Network Isn't There, Become More "Social"

What happens if you have lost contact with people you once knew? I admire what a high school friend Bob did. He reached out to me through my social networking site called LinkedIn. We hadn't talked for more than a decade, but he asked that we get reconnected.

Bob knew I was a networker thanks to my list of contacts on LinkedIn. This is a great way to make a connection with a person who can provide you with an introduction. As I've said, an introduction from a mutual contact is more effective than a cold lead. These types of social networking sites make your sphere of influence very transparent (if you don't hide it in your security settings). At my coffee shop meeting with Bob, I learned he was a social networking expert and was looking for potential clients. I give him credit for asking for exactly what he wanted. Because he was proficient and an old friend, I introduced him to Sam, who needed a researcher for his online company. Bob was hired by my contact. Had my friend applied online at the company's website, it's likely his résumé would never had been reviewed.

Don't forget Facebook. The social networking site's users continue to increase each year. I believe it's now at over 900 million users worldwide. I originally created my profile page to stay in touch with my friends and family. But now, I've transitioned my page to also include coworkers, clients, and even casting directors. I find that it's a great resource for reaching out to people, especially if I am promoting a project that I'm passionate about. With that said, I've kept my profile page professional. I don't have anything embarrassing there that may hurt my future chances for a job or my professional relationships. My Facebook profile page includes pictures and status updates that show me in a positive light, while I engage in an online dialogue with people who I want to stay in touch with.

My "friends" also include media contacts. I can't tell you how powerful Facebook can be if you leverage it properly. When Hurricane Irene swept through Lower Manhattan in August of 2011, it shut down public transportation from subways to airports and trains. This is the first time this has happened in New York City because of a natural disaster. I was in the Big Apple for a speaking engagement for Ascend, a Pan Asian American leadership group, which was canceled because of Irene. As soon as I heard, I wanted to turn around and fly back on the next flight. Unfortunately, that didn't happen. The backlog of travelers from canceled flights made flying back home difficult. I posted a story on Facebook that I was stuck in New York City because of the hurricane. It led to a phone interview for a Seattle TV station, another interview for radio, and then a print interview. I got to tell people about my experience and plug this nonprofit organization. Well, Ascend was thrilled! So, when they rescheduled the event, I was asked to come back.

As I shared with you, my Facebook page is fun, yet professional. I don't believe these two criteria have to be exclusive. Facebook allows me to categorize my list of "friends." I have the option for the whole world to see my friends or put the list on a "limited" access filter, which beefs up my security and my privacy. I can do the same with my postings. I can filter who sees them. I don't post something that I believe a group of "friends" would find unprofessional. It is the Internet after all, which means whatever information makes it online is likely to stay on the web forever.

This reminds me of a story an executive told me about a potential hire his team was about to make for a marketing position at their company. The candidate lost the opportunity because they found some questionable pictures on his MySpace page, another social networking site. That indiscretion cost him a six-figure job! Ouch! Again, think of the Internet as a person. You want to make a good impression. You don't know if Big Brother is watching. Here are the three takeaways:

- Keep it professional.
- Don't upload questionable photos or use potentially damaging language.
- It's the Internet after all, which means forever.

I Don't Know Anyone

Let's go to an extreme. Let's say you don't know anyone or you actually just stepped "off the boat." If you're an immigrant, you have a sponsor who helped you come to America, which is typically a friend or a family member. My mom and Lola have been the sponsors for my family members and excellent advocates for getting them jobs. But what if you really don't know anyone or your sponsor has limited connections? Let's say you are a political refugee from your native country and the US government gave you asylum. Now what?

Al Sugiyama has been an activist for more than forty years and the founding director of the Center for Career Alternatives (CCA) in Seattle, a nonprofit that was established in 1979. It aims to help low-income workers of all races, typically immigrants and refugees, with education, employment, and job training. Al said that most immigrants can find contacts at places like CCA. (CCA has since merged with another organization, Sea Mar, which operates health clinics all over the state.)

Al said big cities typically attract a diverse group of people moving into a central location. This also means there are resources available that cater to immigrants and minorities to help them with employment or job training. In Seattle, there's the Asian Counseling and Referral Service (ACRS), which also offers on-the-job training. In Seattle, where people care about the environment, there's even a grassroots organization with that theme: Got Green. It focuses on helping low-income people and communities of color get access to the green movement and its economy through education, which can also help them get green jobs. Another resource on a national scale is the National Domestic Workers Alliance (www.domesticworkers.org). This is just the start.

I also learned after attending the 4th Annual National Immigrant Integration Conference in Seattle in 2011 that immigrants—even those with skills—usually don't know how to transition to the workforce. For one thing, their résumés are often several pages long. (In this country, the standard is one page.) Plus, their professional license often doesn't meet the requirement qualifications in this country.

I interviewed Monique Caintic on a social injustice story for the *IE*. She said her mother, who was a registered nurse in the Philippines for thirty-five years, was not able to practice at the same level when she came to America. Her degree only allowed her to be a licensed practical nurse, an assistant to a registered nurse. According to Monique, the job meant less pay and less prestige.

"It reveals a larger systemic issue that people of color, especially foreign-born persons, are in fact not respected and our education not deemed credible. My mom worked so hard for her degrees and deserves to be working in a job that matches her level of intellect."

As a result, an immigrant holding an entry-level position may actually be overqualified, so don't underestimate immigrants. According to Marcia Drew Hohn, the director of the Public Education Institute for The Immigrant Learning Center, immigrants are more likely to be entrepreneurs than most Americans. "Immigrants have the courage and the drive to take risks. They give up a lot to come to this country. They leave everything familiar behind to get ahead in a new land. Sometimes, it's a better economic option." Marcia says not only are we seeing immigrants in the healthcare space and service industry, they are also running companies that are household names: Google, Yahoo!, YouTube, and PayPal. These companies were founded by immigrants, according to research done by Richard Herman.

How do you get started in the entrepreneur track? While The Immigrant Learning Center is based in Massachusetts, you should find an organization near your city that caters to promoting immigrants as an asset to this country.

But what if you're a college student from any background who's about to enter the job force for the first time? Are you entering a new industry where you don't have any connections? Well, it's time to get out and meet people or:

Get an Internship

If you are a college student who wants to break into a particular field, your diploma alone won't get you the job. So, start looking at internships in your chosen profession. You may have to go online or make a phone call to find the internship requirements for a particular company. What is the internship deadline? What's the process? Research right away. You may also go to the career-counseling department at your university to ask for assistance or go to the library.

Just don't wait until your senior year to start looking for an internship. Real go-getters and focused students may already have had at least one internship by then. Procrastinating only backs you into a corner. What happens if you do the internship your senior year and learn you don't like that industry? You find out "this isn't for me." It's better that you discover this now rather than later.

Worse case scenario: What happens if you don't get into the internship you want? You missed the deadline. And, in just a few months, you graduate with zero work experience. Most companies won't take on college graduates for their internship programs because they have another name for that—a full-time job. As I shared with you, companies that pay higher salaries are reluctant to hire people with no work experience in their industry.

I think I made my point. Get an internship!

Now, you'll be lucky if you do find paid internships, but most don't pay.

"You are telling me I have to work for free?"

"Yes!" Think of it as an investment. This is your time to stand out. Exceed expectations. Companies will take notice. Do you come to work on time? Do you listen and take directions well? Do you follow through on your projects efficiently with no or minimal errors? Do you have a good attitude?

An internship is almost like a job interview. It allows hiring managers to look at you and make one of two determinations:

Thank goodness this person is just an intern, and it's *temporary.*

Wow! This intern is solid. How can we make room for him or her to be part of our team on a *permanent* basis?

The latter is obviously better. Companies are weird. They don't want to hire someone without experience because they don't want to train you on the job. Your lack of productivity costs them money. They expect you to do the job. That's what you're hired to do.

By the same token, how can you get job experience if no one wants to take a chance? That's why you want to stand out in a memorable way during your internship.

A friend of mine, Lee, was offered a sales rep position right after his internship at Nabisco. During his internship, he worked directly under the regional manager, who had him work with district managers and individual sales reps.

When Lee went out on the field with the sales reps, he didn't just observe. He also asked smart questions. "Tell me how you would sell the store sales manager about getting better aisle space for Nabisco products?"

(To give you some background, the placement of products you see at the grocery stores has a purpose and a strategy. The grocery business is very competitive, and each company fights for prime display locations for their products. Companies know product placement can make or break them. Nobody wants to be at the very back of the store where there is little foot traffic.)

Aside from his well-thought-out questions, sales reps liked Lee's initiative as he was also willing to do the unglamorous part of the job, like coming in early to set up the display ads in grocery stores. The sales reps appreciated the extra help.

Lee earned the regional manager's trust, and he was the company's representative for the Ladies Professional Golf Association, a national golf tournament for which Nabisco was one of the sponsors. Lee's job was to collect consumer information. Managers gave Lee no direction on how to get people to fill out a survey during the golf tournament.

With his own initiative, Lee set up a putting green at his booth. In order to play, you first had to fill out a survey. People lined up at his booth, knowing if they putted the ball into the hole with three tries, they got a *free* goodie bag filled with Nabisco products. Who could say no to Oreos?

His idea turned out to be a great success. He left the golf tournament with stacks of surveys filled with valuable customer information. And not only did Lee earn a glowing recommendation from his managers, Nabisco offered him a sales rep position.

But, Lee turned the offer down. Because he had a glowing recommendation from Nabisco and real-work experience, which he was able to explain in detail, a pharmaceutical company offered him $20,000 more and a company car. How's that for a graduation present? A job! Imagine having two companies fighting for you, and you haven't even graduated from college yet.

Well, what about if you are in a situation where you can't turn the clock back? What if you're in a different place in your life where a college internship just isn't an option.

You're Never Too Old to Work

Let me introduce you to my Lola. She came here to America in her fifties, just a few years shy of retirement for many Americans. When Lola first arrived in this country, the management at the hotel where my mother had first gave her a job in the laundry department. If that sounds humble or depressing, please realize that for the first time in her life, she was going to receive a steady paycheck and work for a company with benefits. In the Philippines, her other jobs, such as sewing or hand washing the neighbors' clothing, were always paid under the table with no form of job security and no benefits.

Since my mom couldn't drive Lola to work, she had to learn how to navigate the bus system without knowing the city well. To this day, I remember the three of us spending an entire day showing Lola how to use the local public transportation.

Lola even needed instructions on how to use the timecard, and my mother showed her how prior to her first day at work. Mom didn't want Lola's employers wasting time with her timecard when it was better spent showing Lola how to operate the laundry machines.

Not long after taking this first job, Lola took a second one at a retirement home helping to clean up the dining room. Her English and education were limited, so Lola gladly accepted the work. All she could think about was how long she could stay healthy to help support her nine children and some forty grandchildren all over the world, while still paying her bills.

I felt bad for Lola, since her two jobs didn't allow her time to attend "English as a Second Language" night school. Learning the language on the job at her age was challenging. But in the larger picture, this was nothing more than a petty annoyance. I know for a fact that she would not have wanted to be anywhere else.

She knew how fortunate she was to get a job with benefits at her age. I will always be grateful for my adoptive country for providing people like my Lola with a second chance in life. Eventually she was even offered three other jobs, which would have been unheard of in the Philippines. There, potential employers wouldn't look twice at her résumé.

Great Pay, Lack Passion, Making that Switch

You can do what fashion couture designer, Luly Yang did. I met her at a benefit dinner for the Tsunami survivors of Japan, following the March 2011 catastrophe caused by a massive 8.9-magnitude earthquake.

An immigrant from Taiwan, Luly didn't realize her real passion until later on in her life and in an entirely different career. For nine years, Luly worked as a graphic designer and spent time in the architectural space. She didn't know her real calling until another graphic designer suggested she enter a fashion show contest sponsored by a paper company. Luly created two butterfly dresses that would change her life.

"It was interesting that I chose a butterfly design since butterflies symbolize change and metamorphosis. The process of making that dress was me saying to myself, 'It's time to get out of my current job and go into what I've always wanted to do.'"

The transition didn't take place overnight. She continued to work part-time, and then as a freelance graphic designer for one year while she was building her business. Luly then took out a home-equity loan and rented a modest studio to work on her real passion: designing and creating dresses. She needed to keep costs down during this time, especially since she was still a novice and this was a start-up. Her story differs from Ben's, owner of Cheezburger, who had some work experience with an online start-up. For the first three years as a self-taught fashion designer, Luly carved out time to travel and learn from other experts in the fashion industry. She networked and wasn't afraid to ask questions.

"I didn't have a business foundation, even though I had grown up in a family who did. I had never run a business myself. So my expectations were different." Luly added, "I expected to do so many different things on my own. And, I learned that I really needed either a consultant or people who complemented me because I couldn't do it all. I'm good at certain things so I should focus on them."

Luly surrounded herself with a supportive cast who believed in her. Today, as I drive to work at RealSelf, I pass by her boutique on 4th Avenue in Seattle, and am in awe of the dresses she's designed and created. Her bridal line is my favorite. Luly showed me that you can switch careers later in life and be successful with the right attitude and good people around you. Some of her celebrity clients include TV personality Vanessa Minnillo, Mona Lee Locke (former TV news anchor and wife of the former governor of Washington State who is the current US Ambassador to China), and me.

Luly made a daring life-changing decision that paid off, and her life is better for it. Luly said, "I have used this simple statement for our Internet and marketing message: 'Sometimes, life is better than the dream,' which means you can make your life better by living your dream. But this, I believe, only happens if you do what you love."

Let's say you have the language and educational skills, but you're not following your passion.

Say Cheese

If you've wanted to switch your career and don't know how, you can simply start by getting yourself out there more and surrounding yourself with the people in the industry you aspire to enter.

This is a time to widen your sphere and start practicing how to smile because you're going to be meeting a lot of new people, shaking hands, and smiling. How about joining a professional organization in this field and volunteering for their pet causes? Every industry from environmental to fashion supports humanitarian causes, and you can volunteer and rub elbows with people in your industry of choice.

When you put yourself out there, you'll end up meeting new people with various contacts and skill sets. You'll also be helping out others, which makes others want to help you.

Take this story, for instance. I attended a charity event that raised money for the *IE*, a nonprofit media organization. I didn't attend the event to look for a job, but to support the cause.

I didn't know a lot of the guests. A journalist friend of mine, James Tabafunda, knew just about every key decision maker in the room because he had interviewed them at one time or another. He introduced me to many of these people, including Michael, the owner of a Seattle newspaper. He and I made a connection. We're both in media. His is the newspaper world. Mine is online. While we didn't get a chance to talk in-depth, I did give him an elevator pitch. "Hi, I'm Maureen Francisco. I'm working in various aspects of the media from being a freelance writer to writing a nonfiction book. I've been a TV reporter and anchor and a reality show contestant. I enjoy projects that empower women, young professionals, and children." That was enough to give him a window into my professional life. We did exchange business cards. A day later, I followed up to let him know that we should keep in touch.

Well, we did. Michael and I met up for coffee. And, in our meeting, I learned he was putting on the Renton International Festival, an event celebrating diversity. I told him I'm active in community-based programs that enable women, children, and immigrants to achieve their best. He knew I had broadcasting experience, and he was looking for an emcee during the ribbon-cutting ceremony. I agreed to be his co-emcee.

On that stage at the first Renton's International Festival, I stood in front of the media, politicians, business leaders, the Miss Vietnamese Washington Organization, and Miss Washington; all of them were people I had never met. My contacts just got larger.

From that festival, I ended up making friends with the director of the Miss Vietnamese Washington Organization, Samantha. From our friendship, I learned she's forty and a mother of two. Well, Samantha has the body and face of a twenty-one-year-old, and I wanted to know her secret. She attributed her youthful appearance to drinking plenty of water, eating in proportion, and avoiding alcohol and smoking. I did a blog about her at RealSelf. Typically our blogs are about trends and news regarding aesthetic surgery. Samantha's story gave our consumers a different perspective on beauty.

Getting out there led to relationships with Michael and Samantha where we ended up working together, but not all introductions will. Well, maybe not the first time.

Don't Burn a Bridge

I recall applying for a principal role in a commercial about helping people who found themselves with some money woes. I met with the executive producer, Marcello, where I personally handed him an audition CD and résumé. I thought the meeting went well, and, for sure, I would get the part. Wrong. He and the client went in a different direction.

I sent Marcello a professional e-mail thanking him for the opportunity and saying I would love to work with him in the future.

Two years went by and out of the blue, Marcello sent me an e-mail. He asked me if I'd be interested in being a principal for a commercial he was working on. My "look" fit the role perfectly, and I didn't need an audition CD like last time. Instead, Marcello gave me the principal role in a commercial that aired throughout the Northwest on almost every major cable network. I got primetime face time. That role was not for amateurs.

So why didn't Marcello hire me the first time? Maybe it was because of my height? Maybe my looks? Maybe (fill in the blanks)? Regardless, he had still kept my information on file.

Imagine if I had sent Marcello an e-mail that said something like "You made a big mistake by not hiring me." I'm sure Marcello would've deleted my contact information ASAP.

This example could apply for the job you want. You're educated, you're talented, and you know you are good, yet you keep getting rejected. You've always followed-up on interviews with a "thank you" for the opportunity e-mail or handwritten card.

Let's try something different. I'd still send the "thank-you" e-mail, but also ask for feedback on why you didn't get the job.

Listen to that person's suggestions, especially if the person who's giving you the constructive criticism has real credibility. Is it someone who interviews job applicants frequently? Take those suggestions from people with the knowledge and work on them. So, at the next job interview, you've put in the work and you hear, "When can you start?"

Home Sweet Home

You always want to keep your options open. When I was a TV reporter and anchor throughout the country, I still stayed in contact with key decision makers in the Seattle news business. Some were hiring managers who I had worked with during my internships, while others were professors who kept up with their star students and would know about potential job openings, as well as other colleagues and relationships in the know.

Within weeks of moving back to Seattle after a five-year absence, I found a position as a freelance TV reporter for a cable TV station. While I went from one market to the next, my end goal was to be a TV reporter in my own backyard. To make sure I had "face time" with these people, I reached out with a simple e-mail or a holiday card or a birthday greeting. It was enough "face time" for them to not forget me. So when I moved back for good, a relationship had been established. I felt confident asking, "Can you make room for me in your newsroom?"

So, always keep the door open, especially if you're a college student who is eager to leave your hometown in search of adventure. As you get older, things change in life, and the thrill of moving to another "new" city isn't as enticing as it once was. Needs change. Do you want to start a family? If so, do you want to do it near your family and friends? Do you have aging parents who need to be taken care of? Whatever the reason for coming back "home" later, it's a good idea to periodically reach out to people who can be a resource for you at that time. That way you can do what I did two weeks after moving back "home." I was confident to ask for a job with people who still knew me.

CHAPTER FIVE

Improve Your Language Skills

I came here to America when I was just five years old. I can remember that day as though it was yesterday. I was scared flying to a foreign land, leaving my friends and extended family behind and the only country I knew.

At that time, I spoke very little English. In the Philippines, with its longtime American influence, many people speak a combination of English and our native tongue, Tagalog. While I was in kindergarten, my mother often spoke to me in "Taglish," as we called it, and so I knew a little English but couldn't express myself very well.

In America, I really struggled with the language. In my first grade class, I was unable to understand what my teacher was saying. She was literally speaking a foreign language. My classmates didn't make the transition to this new country any easier. They'd make fun of me since I couldn't clearly articulate my thoughts and feelings. This was tough for my mother to watch as she knew that I was a bright child.

Hoping to make the transition more comfortable for me, Mom sat on a bench outside of the classroom, sometimes staying all day in case I needed her, and I could see her through the window from my desk. This episode is one of my fondest childhood memories, because it showed me how much my mother loved me. She sat there patiently with no reading material to help pass time. When the lunch bell rang, we'd eat together, and after school we walked home together.

She sat outside my classroom for almost a week until the principal asked why she was staying. She explained that we had just immigrated to America and I had a tough time understanding the language, and that if I needed her to translate, she was right there to help me. The principal assured my mother I would be okay without her.

On our walk home that night, my mom told me of her conversation with the principal and that she would be dropping me off from now on and returning home. She said in Tagalog, "I promise you will be okay."

I wanted to fit in with the other students, but the language barrier made it tough. I found myself playing alone during recess. For many of my classmates, it was the first time they had seen someone who didn't look like them. The meanest ones would chant, "Japanese, Chinese, dirty knees, look at these." On the word Japanese, the kids pulled their eyes up. On the word Chinese, they pulled their eyes down.

But, my classmates didn't realize I was neither Japanese nor Chinese. I was Filipino. I thought, perhaps, these kids think all Asians and Pacific Islanders looked alike. We don't. From the start, the chant didn't make sense to me. So, when the "dirty knees" part came up, and the kids would pull their shirt away from their body and look down their chest, I thought it was weird. They looked ridiculous!

Unfortunately, my English didn't improve as fast as the class progressed. I fell behind. By the end of winter, it was clear that my first-grade year would not be completed at Lake Grove Elementary School. I had to go to a different school.

English as a Second Language

The school district classified me as an "English as a second language student," or ESL student. It wasn't a bad thing. It just meant I needed more help with my English than most students. My mother understood it differently. She thought that the school saw me as a "special needs" student. She cried and took the news personally, as if she had somehow failed. In the Philippines, I had stood out from my peers in kindergarten. She didn't want anyone to see me as having "special" needs in a negative way.

My new school was Mirror Lake Elementary. It was not within walking distance, so I had to take a school bus. That was a first for me. Back in the Philippines, curbside transportation—where a bus picked a person up directly from her house and dropped her off afterward—was reserved for the wealthy. So, this new accommodation both surprised and pleased us.

As an ESL student, I had two teachers and two classes. The first half of the day was dedicated to helping me improve my English. The class consisted of other ESL students. Now I found myself in the company of other people of various racial backgrounds. These students came from Vietnam, Laos, and Cambodia. The second half of my day was spent with the other students who spoke English as their first language.

With the two classes, a lunch break, and three recesses, my day went fast, and so did my progress. My learning curve at my new school looked like the stock market in the late nineties—going up, up, and up. As with most children, my mind worked like a sponge, absorbing so much information with such ease. Looking back, I should have learned how to speak Spanish, enrolled in dance classes, taken on gymnastics, singing, and more because when I tried to learn those things later on in life, I struggled. My mind as a child was like sticky notes on the refrigerator—*one more thing to remember . . . one more thing not to forget.*

As I said, my dad wanted me to accelerate my English, so he made a rule that only English could be spoken at home. My mother and I stopped conversing in Tagalog in the house.

Practice, Practice, Practice

I immersed myself in English during my childhood years. At home, I watched the television news and listened carefully to how the reporters and anchors spoke the language. I found myself repeating what they said out loud. I had no idea it would plant a seed that later on in my life would lead to a career in journalism.

In fact, when I watched TV programs or movies, I turned the living room into a classroom setting where the TV became the teacher. I listened to how people articulated their words and the pitch and tone of their voice. When a question was asked, the tone of the voice goes up. And, when someone wants something emphasized, they put a lot of "oomph" behind that word. This helped my presentation skills later on in life—I learned how to not speak in a monotone.

So, if you really want to work on your English, not only listen to the words being spoken on the screen, but read them, too, by having the subtitles on. I used to do that in high school when I was taking Spanish and I wanted to learn how the words would be translated into English. Nearly every DVD movie and many TV shows offer subtitles as options. That's another way to continually learn and practice.

I read tons of books too and was involved in the reading club. I'll have to admit that I did it because for every book you read, the school rewarded you with a prize, from a pencil to a bookmark. But, while the prizes kept me going to the library to check out new books, the constant reading helped me improve my language skills and spelling as well. When I was in the fourth grade, I became the fourth grade Spelling Bee Champion.

I also participated in Girl Scouts. Again, I surrounded myself with other English-speaking kids. And my English was put to the test when I had to sell cookies to strangers door to door. People would ask me, "What's your favorite box of cookies?"

I had to tell the customer, "Shortbread is my favorite because it's not too sweet like the Caramel deLites. Would you like to buy a box?"

Having a conversation with adults really forced me out of my comfort zone.

In high school, I strove to improve my English. I was on the debate team and enrolled in Honors English. I was surrounded by my peers who appreciated writing, debating, and reading. They accelerated my overall English skills.

I encourage you to surround yourself with people who speak better English than you do to pick up their good habits. If they speak English well, it's likely you will too. If you are around people who talk in street slang, it's very easy to pick up that habit as well.

You Will Never Be Perfect—Just Better

So, the learning never stopped for me after I graduated from college. I even hired a voice coach while I was a reporter in Savannah, Georgia. She had coached many on-air personalities who were working at various networks. I flew all the way to Chicago to work with this voice talent to help make my delivery more conversational, as if I were speaking to a friend. It's not good enough just to know the language; the delivery is equally as important in the TV business or in general. And, I was willing to make that investment. You don't have to spend money on a plane ticket and voice lessons like I did. But are you willing to make an investment in yourself?

However, it was when I took acting classes that I found my authentic voice. They allowed me the creative freedom to take risks and be uninhibited. I spoke the way I felt. I didn't think. I just did it. All the training and practicing English allowed me to be in a place to stop thinking, and just do. I then applied this lesson to other parts of my life. I now go for it and take risks. Nothing is too big to go after!

I asked Dee Wallace in an interview for a women's magazine, "What's the biggest mistake actors make?" Dee is the star of *E.T.: The Extra-Terrestrial* and has more than 100 film credits to her name. She said it's tough for actors to be authentic. "I think we're afraid to B.S. From the time we're very small, we are taught to conform to society and do what's right. To really honor your truthful feeling is a scary thing. We're taught to be very careful of what we say because society is not going to accept you. People are going to judge you."

Dee shared with me that when she wasn't being "authentic" professionally, it cost her film roles; personally, it often robbed her of her happiness, when she was trying to be someone she's not.

Find Your Voice

It's not just actors who struggle to be authentic, but also people in general, especially immigrants who are afraid they may say the wrong thing or say something in a way that isn't acceptable. People are afraid to be judged and rejected. I better understood Dee's quote when I had dinner with one of the vice presidents of NBCUniversal, Bruno Singh, at an Ascend event. He shared with me that as an immigrant from India working in the information technology space, there's a stereotype that people like him are "boring." He said he took lessons similar to those taught in an acting class that allowed him to find his authentic voice and always be true to himself. Act on what your gut feels, not what you think others expect. Bruno doesn't have to be the typically quiet Asian male, if that's not him. He can be as gregarious, humorous, and candid a person in a professional setting as he is with his friends and family. As a result, he told me he's able to influence and lead people more effectively by just being himself.

If you do speak English well, but you find yourself rigid and being a bit "blah," I do encourage you to explore acting classes. They give you the creative freedom in a "safe" place to be yourself and trust your gut in any given situation. I must say that it has helped improve my presentation and impromptu speaking abilities.

Today, I'm asked to emcee events and be a keynote speaker not only because of my unique background, but also because I tell my story in a unique way—my authentic voice. Organizers of these events can ask a lot of people with a similar background to be the co-emcee or keynote speaker. But what sets my story apart is my authentic voice. It's the way I package myself to the public that can't be replicated by anyone else.

A friend, Thach Nguyen, who came to this country from Vietnam with only the clothes on his back, told me he has worked really hard on improving his language skills. English is his second language and he speaks with an accent. Despite his success story—he was a millionaire real estate tycoon by twenty-seven—he always felt he had something to prove despite living in this country for years and being successful. Yet, he felt like he didn't quite fit in. "I still feel a little bit like other Americans are above me. I'm trying to speak more professionally and make sure I don't sound or look stupid. I'm trying to be equal with them. You feel like you are never good enough. The problem is there's someone richer, smarter, and faster than you. I noticed I was driven by that and never felt peaceful with where I was."

He finally shook off those low "self-worth" feelings later on in his life. As a philanthropist today, Thach is repeatedly asked to be a keynote speaker for various organizations. I've even asked him to speak at my sponsored events. I'm drawn to Thach because of his story and his authentic voice—accent and all.

I encourage you to find your voice. Again, it may sound simple, but it took me a while to own mine.

Create Your Safe Environment

If acting is out of your comfort zone and you do want to take your speaking abilities to another level, how about the Toastmasters Club? It's a nonprofit organization that helps people with their public speaking. I'm an alum. Since I spent five years working all over the country as a TV reporter and an anchor, did I really need the class? I'm humble enough to say I'm never too good to practice. I still have an appetite to learn and improve. My favorite exploration at the Toastmasters Club was speaking about topics on the spot, which really kept me on my toes.

While I'm no longer in Toastmasters, I am part of Ascend. I get a lot of practice speaking and sharing with this organization. I often find myself surrounded by peers who speak English well and for whom English wasn't their first language. Some are immigrants; many are born here. It's helpful to network with professionals and share my journey in a safe environment. People who go there either want to be mentored by other Pan Asian American leaders or they want to act as a coach to young professionals. When you are in the learning frame of mind, you need a safe, supportive environment because you'll make mistakes.

Just remember, you have to keep practicing regularly if you want to improve. You are not going to get better without putting some work behind it. As you read from my examples, it doesn't to have to be in a classroom setting.

Use Your "Practice" Time Wisely

I have a neighbor who came from the Philippines to America nearly a decade ago, and she still hasn't been able to secure her driver's license.

It's because she has a tough time passing the written part of the driving test. I know she'd ace the actual driving test. But, she can't get there until she passes the written exam. I must say that I don't see her putting much work into improving her written language skills. She doesn't read English books or watch American movies with subtitles. I do see her singing karaoke with English subtitles regularly, but that's not helping her with the written portion of the driving test. This is where her practice time isn't being used to her advantage.

Now, she's great at belting out almost every Celine Dion song. Whenever we go to a party and there's karaoke, she is the center of attention. People often comment on how much her English has improved. But, singing karaoke hasn't helped her get behind the wheel. Her inability to drive has hindered her quality of life. While she is one of my favorite people and I love her dearly, I know if she got a driver's license, it would give her so much more freedom and flexibility with her schedule.

Don't Lose Your Native Tongue

Here I've been saying, practice, practice, and practice your English, but it's also good to not forget your native tongue. While my dad's intentions were good when he made me speak only English at home, he didn't do me any favors later on in life. Vanna Novak is the president and owner of Speak to Persuade. She is a communication expert and works with Fortune 500 companies. She says that it's critical to learn how to speak and write English well in this country, especially if you want to work in corporate America, but knowing more than one language is an asset. "The timing is really good right now for second-language employees, especially Asians. We see more of our larger corporations working globally, and a lot of them are going into the Asian markets: China, Vietnam, Korea, India, and the Philippines." Unfortunately, my Tagalog went by the wayside.

My English had progressed rapidly enough that I returned to Lake Grove Elementary School for my third-grade year. But I still spoke with a Filipino accent. Again, that's not a bad thing according to Vanna. "Our ears are getting more accustomed to hearing different accents. Today, it depends on the job you're in and the qualifications you bring to the job. If, however, the accent gets in the way of people understanding what you're saying, then that's definitely going to work against you. I have to easily be able to understand you."

You're Not from Around Here?

What happens if your accent doesn't improve? Andy Yip admits that he still speaks with a heavy accent despite being in America for more than fifteen years. While his accent has gotten better over the years,

Andy says he has embraced it as just part of who he is that makes him authentic.

"My personal skills supplement my inability to speak fluently. I excel in face-to-face meetings, where my facial expressions, my gestures, and my posture help express what I'm saying."

As I mentioned earlier, I remember when a boss didn't find my accent charming at all. I was working in Yakima. During my first one-to-one with my news director, he said that my accent would get in the way of my acceleration to bigger markets. He was wrong! In five years, I made it to the Seattle market. The accent never got in the way. There are quite a few big on-air talent with accents. I see that it adds to their on-air personal charm. And, as there are more channels and more diverse talent on the air, accents aren't a bad thing anymore—unless of course, you work in telemarketing or behind the scenes where people hear you but don't see you.

I did attempt to go back and relearn how to speak Tagalog as an adult. I enrolled in a class at a community center. It was tough to reprogram my mind to be open to a new language. I felt like I was in first grade all over again as I couldn't keep up with my teacher. But, I kept at it every week that entire summer. Of course, I know it takes more than one summer class to improve a native language. But, I just got super frustrated that my mind wasn't able to absorb my native tongue like a sponge.

Fortunately, I was not in a career that required me to speak Tagalog. My career was thriving because I kept working hard to improve my English. Now, if you are at a place where you need to brush up on English or another language, you can find language classes either at your local college, community center, or even an agency that specializes in helping immigrants. For example, ACRS in Seattle is a nonprofit organization that helps immigrants, refugees, and American-born people with classes from learning how to speak English to becoming US citizens. Go online and do your research to find more information on classes near you. There's bound to be more than one resource available to help you schedule a language class.

I've come a long way since arriving in this country without speaking the language well. While Andy came here from Hong Kong when he was fifteen years old, he did know how to speak some English, but said that he still struggled. He knew British English, which is very different from American English. Not just the language, but the entire school system is different. "It took a full quarter for me to integrate into class activities. The whole system is different from what we have in Asia. There, everything is very orderly. You always stay in the same class, and it is the teachers who run around from classroom to classroom."

While Andy struggled in English and had to go to an ESL class like me, he was far more advanced in math and science and way ahead of his peers. "Most people in Hong Kong have grown up with the mindset that Hong Kong is the world's financial center. In school, the emphasis is on numbers, and finances are just second nature to us."

Yet Andy never lost his ability to speak his native tongue, Chinese, and along the way he was able to learn other languages too. "I speak Mandarin, Cantonese, English, and Japanese." He shared with me that since he knew how to speak a few Asian languages, picking up another one was easier compared to someone like me who stopped after learning one language. It's just like exercising. If you stop exercising for years, you become sedentary. That's what happened with my mind when it came to speaking multiple languages. The muscles to formulate new sentences in another language became sedentary. Fortunately for Andy, his ability to fluently speak four languages makes him extremely marketable.

Andy's story reminds me of my cousin Jeff, whose family emigrated from the Philippines to Montreal, Canada, when he was around ten years old. Jeff's parents practiced Tagalog with him at home. Jeff knew English from living for ten years in the Philippines where English is mandatory in grade school. So, when his family moved to Montreal, where French is the common language, he was able to pick it up easily. I could never understand the American public school system, where being able to speak another language is only a requirement to graduate in high school. Why wait that long? Children's minds are more malleable to new languages at a younger age.

Don't Skip Those English Classes

Fifth Degree black belt Marcello Alonso learned the hard way about what happens when English is not your first or even your second language. When he came to this country from Brazil to teach Brazilian Jiu Jitsu, he had a tough time speaking English, and he said it was his fault. Marcello said, "I mimicked to speak. I was frustrated and sad because I didn't go to English classes back home that my dad paid for."

Because Marcello couldn't speak the language, people often thought he was an illegal immigrant. To overcome the discrimination he faced regularly, Marcello would quickly tell people, "I give classes to police and Special Forces soliders." This changed the way they looked at him.

Marcello struggled to adjust to his new homeland. And, it didn't help that he came to this country as an adult, which made it harder to adapt and to learn a new language and new customs.

While Marcello eventually became his own boss and started one of the first Brazilian Jiu Jitsu schools in the Northwest, he would've struggled working in a corporate environment where being able to speak English well is a requirement, especially when you have to influence a group.

Vanna says, "Being able to speak out when it counts and to be able to express yourself fluently will help you to articulate your ideas in a meaningful way. This will help you have the kind of impact that can make a difference. And, you will easily be perceived as a leader. By a leader, I mean you are a 'thought' leader. You generate ideas that people not only want to listen to but want to put into action. Those that generate positive results."

So, Vanna says it's more than knowing the mechanics of the English language and pronunciation, but also being able to put words and thoughts together in an original way. This can be done at home with parents coaching their children to speak their own mind. It can be as simple as healthy conversations around the dinner table. While my dad encouraged me to speak in English, my own opinions didn't seem to matter much. His voice made it tough for me to express myself and to formulate my own thoughts.

As a result, I was shy as a kid and really didn't speak much in class. I followed the quiet-child style and was a "good" kid until college, where I was encouraged to speak my mind in my communication classes. That was a huge confidence boost for me. I found that the more talkative I became, the more confident I also became as a person.

While Marcello wasn't able to articulate his thoughts in English to others, he worked in a field where his "body language" spoke for him.

His background, reputation, and relationship with Carlson Gracie Jr., whose father helped develop the moves of Brazilian Jiu Jitsu, helped Marcelo be known as "master" in his community. His technical fighting skills and an encyclopedia of knowledge of mixed martial arts (MMA) allows him to train fighters for competitions. You mention the name Marcelo in the MMA community, and right away people say nothing but good things about him. Today, Marcelo has schools in Washington State, Oregon, and Alaska.

Don't Judge Someone by Their Looks

You've read Marcelo's story about the discrimination he faced because of his ethnic appearance. Ironically, because I'm Filipino, I get the "reverse" discrimination, as do many second-generation Japanese and Chinese. People automatically assume I speak Tagalog and speak it well, just as they assume because you look Chinese, you speak Mandarin. Since I've forgotten most of my Tagalog, I suffer discrimination for the fact that I don't speak a second language. Some people even think that I'm undereducated, or I am asked, "Why can't you speak Tagalog anymore?" Then I have to explain that in my childhood my English-speaking dad was adamant about the English-only rule at home. So, I and many other immigrant children from other countries are stereotyped in this manner. I can still say a few words in Tagalog to get by; it helps that most Filipinos speak "Taglish." So, I can usually guess what the person is trying to say.

When I'm asked to emcee at events where the audience is primarily Filipinos, I know I disappoint them when I say I won't be able to converse the entire time in Tagalog. I regret this part of my life that I let slip by. It's not because I am not proud of my culture. I just simply stopped practicing.

When I do have the time, I will go back and relearn Tagalog so I can pass this on to my children.

Texting: LOL!

This isn't a laughing matter. I discovered the acronym LOL a few years ago—Laugh Out Loud. Now, with so many people walking around with mobile phones, I find that more prefer to text than actually speak over the phone. If you are trying to improve your language skills, I really don't recommend taking the shortcut and always texting. How is this improving your ability to speak? And, I don't encourage you to create your own text dictionary with your own spelling rules. This is a text I received from someone who is trying to learn English: "Maureen, how r u? U wanna grab dinner?"

I get it that it's faster to take shortcuts when you text, but I find that this person is making it a habit even in e-mail communications. She is not practicing writing better English. She is accepting "shortcuts" that will undermine her chances of getting ahead in business and in life.

This also applies to my cousins who are still trying to understand the English language but are taking shortcuts to communicate with me by texting with misspellings and using poor grammar. How you speak and write on a regular basis becomes your normal style of communicating.

So, please, there's no reason to LOL when your inability to speak and write well is costing you an advancement in your career and life.

CHAPTER SIX

Success Is a 24-Hour-a-Day, 365-Day-a-Year Job

"It is a lot later than you think" is a quote I've heard from my friend Wally. I came to understand more of what he meant in my mid-thirties. As I was rummaging through my memory box from my college years, I came across a list of things I wanted to do before I died, like visiting Europe, being on a reality show, or being a published author. I created that list right after I graduated from college. I was now pleasantly surprised when I checked off what I had already done. There were more check marks than blank spaces next to my list of things. While I should be proud of the things I did accomplish, I felt my conscience tapping me on the shoulder, saying, "How are you utilizing your time on this earth? Who are you focusing on? What are you focusing on? And, are those things a good use of your time?" It made me realize that time is so precious. How did those years fly by so fast?

Overnight Success Doesn't Happen Overnight

Over lunch, I heard Richard Cho's story about how he became the first Asian American to be a general manager of a major sports franchise. His story reminded me of the quote, "Overnight success doesn't happen overnight." It takes years of hard work and pure determination. The former Washington resident came back to Seattle to accept an award by the Robert Chinn Foundation as an Asian Hall of Fame honoree for his achievements in the NBA.

At the time of this interview, he's the current general manager of the Charlotte Bobcats—a success story that took some twists and turns. "It was definitely worth the sacrifice," he said.

A Burmese immigrant and a native of Federal Way, Washington, Richard and I went to the same high school, except he graduated years before me. He then attended Washington State University and received an engineering degree. From there, he worked as an engineer for Boeing for the next five years. But, it wasn't his calling.

After work, he was often found playing on a basketball team or playing tennis, and was on multiple softball teams. "I wasn't that great in any of these sports, but one thing I was good at was competing," Richard said. "I hated to lose and it really bothered me when I did. One night, I realized that my true passion in life was sports, and if at all possible, I needed to do something related to sports." He went on to say, "I did some research into different sports careers and found that a lot of sports agents as well as people in governing bodies like the NBA and NFL had law degrees. So, I quit my job at Boeing and went to law school."

With no family of his own, no children or mortgage, Richard packed up and moved to southern California and went to law school. He was in his late twenties. Richard went from making a steady paycheck to making nothing, which was a real shock for him. It also kicked in his competitive drive, and he swore that failure wasn't an option. While finishing his degree at Pepperdine University School of Law, Richard interned for the NBA's Seattle Sonics. He remembers sleeping on the floor of his brother's one-bedroom apartment for free, and earning $4.80 an hour as an intern. "I was starting from scratch again. It wasn't easy."

As Richard thought about his future and wondered how he'd move up the food chain in a field that was saturated with ex-players, he knew he had to stand out. "I'd better be the first one in the office and the last one to leave," Richard recalled. "I also remember thinking that I needed to learn everything I could about the business, ask a lot of questions, and help out whomever and wherever I could to make myself indispensable."

For those next few years, basketball and its business side became his life. Richard credits his laser-focused attitude and discipline to his parents, who always used their time wisely. His dad worked the graveyard shift at a 7-11, and his mom rode the bus an hour one-way to get to the University of Washington library. Neither parent had much free time, especially since they had an entire family to raise.

Richard received the work experience he needed with the Sonics, from director of basketball affairs to scouting to VP of legal to assistant general manager. Fifteen years after his internship with the team, Richard got the call that he'd been waiting for—an opportunity to be a GM for an NBA team. In 2010, he became the first Asian American general manager for the Portland Trail Blazers. "Life is too short to not do something you love."

. . . And Do Something You're Good At

So, how did Richard, who left a stable, comfortable job at Boeing, make history fifteen years later as the first Asian American general manager of a sports franchise? As you read, he wasn't an overnight success. He committed to making his love of sports and basketball his life, and the hard work paid off. He is also good at what he does.

I was in the same school district as another Asian American man who was interested in sports, like Richard. Unlike him though, James Sun made a commitment during high school. The first Asian American male contestant and a runner-up on season six of *The Apprentice*, James remembers wanting to be on the high-school basketball team. It wasn't an over-the-top dream, but something most boys of that age dream about in school. Here's the problem: James hadn't picked up a basketball until the seventh grade. He was at a clear disadvantage with his peers who had gone to basketball camps and been in basketball leagues. So, every weekend for years, James made basketball his life. "I made a drill out of it. I was so bad that I knew I had to outwork the other guys. I would literally do drills on the weekends by myself. Not just playing for fun, but do drills. My sister sometimes would join me; she wanted the exercise. She'd pass me the ball during each drill, and I'd shoot it."

While James eventually did make it on the varsity high school basketball team, he didn't pursue the sport in college. "In high school, I played against a guy like Michael Dickerson who you knew was going to go pro. And, then I played with other guys like Roberto Bergersen who was really good, but he wouldn't make it to the next level, and that's when I realized I probably wouldn't either. I needed to figure this out."

He did get a handle on it. James likes risks and big rewards. It runs in the family. His father left Korea (despite a comfortable life there) for the opportunities in America, and James thought he should follow in his dad's footsteps. "We arrived at LAX with thirty-five dollars," James said. "He literally took on crazy jobs just to make it because he wanted to experience a different life in a new country. That's the kind of gene pool I come from. That's why I'm an entrepreneur by nature."

James embarked on his own journey. He left Deloitte, one of the world's largest financial advisory and consulting companies, and became an entrepreneur over the next few years of his life. He started several companies, such as GeoPage.com—a location-based company that builds mobile applications. Today, he's the CEO of Pirq, an application that gives you instant deals. Don't you think James used his talents better as an entrepreneur than chasing a half-baked dream of being a professional basketball player?

Your Wake-Up Call

A friend of mine, Ed Bennett, the founder and owner of Bennett Media Studio in New York City, told me a life-changing story about how he viewed his use of time. He admitted he was born with talent and easily picked up playing the piano and the guitar; he also had an eye for photography and was able to process information and put it in context. He just took his gifts for granted and didn't put much effort into anything.

So, while in school at MIT, what do you think he was doing on the weekends? "I was partying," he said. He didn't have the work ethic when it came to his studies. Socializing was more of a priority. But, something happened one Sunday at three o'clock in the morning that changed Ed's life forever. He went to use the bathroom of the library and was surprised to see the tables filled with 70 percent Asians. He recognized one of them, his classmate. "He wasn't as talented as me, but I saw him working hard." From that moment, Ed decided to stop partying and focus his time on achieving his dream of being a media mogul. "I knew if I didn't prioritize my time, my classmate would outwork me and get further ahead. Sadly, he wasn't born with my talent, but had the drive I didn't."

Ed has done well for himself since that "aha" moment. Prior to opening his own studio company, he started VH1 and was vice president of the media giant Viacom. Partying was a dead end in college. Networking and doing well in school became his priority, and talent plus drive made him a big success.

Be Strategic with Your Time, Not Just Busy

So, Ed shaped up his time usage. How about you? What are you doing with your time?

Well, if you don't feel like you're wisely using your time promoting your dream, this is what a college friend, who felt the same way, did. Unfortunately, he did it the wrong way. I do admire him for leaving his teaching position at Washington State and moving to Los Angeles to become an actor. That takes guts. Like Ed and Richard, he also felt like he should be following his dreams. But, he didn't come up with a fail-proof plan. I get it. Not all risky plans are fail proof. But he didn't go to

Hollywood with the idea that "failure isn't an option." For one thing, he didn't have a lot of money saved up. He had tons of college loans to pay off from a double major in teaching and psychology at two universities. And this friend also didn't make any contacts in advance who could make things happen for him.

It's interesting in retrospect that my friend invited me to happy hour and picked my brain. I gave him recommendations of what worked for me and what worked for others taking such risks. After interviewing lots of people who did make it big, I shared with him their insights. Did he follow any of them? *No!*

I told him to apply for an internship at one of the studios to get his foot in the door, and he should do it now before he left for Los Angeles. He could easily fly there for interviews from Washington State and should wait until he secured an internship. At least he could still keep his day job. That's what I did when I pursued my dream of being on a reality show. I wasn't going to make that move just to be more available. It made better financial sense to just fly there when I had big auditions so I could continue working my day job.

Instead, my friend got goo-goo eyes when a start-up magazine offered him an editor's position. Unfortunately, it came with no pay. Ed, the guy who started VH1, said my friend fell prey to those who make a living off of other people's dreams. That's typical of Hollywood.

Since his bank account was bleeding money and his parents couldn't help out financially, I suggested that he get a job as a bartender or waiter to pay for the bare minimums like headshots and acting classes when he made that move. Being an actor is an expensive venture. And, it takes years to make it. Until then, he should've been asking himself daily, "How do I keep feeding this dream? What do I need? Money. To pay rent, eat, buy gas. Do I have any income coming in? No. What do I need to do to make sure I have a steady paycheck? Get a job that pays."

My friend didn't take any part-time jobs while in Los Angeles and instead focused his energy on the start-up magazine. This position didn't support him and his dream, and he couldn't even pay for his headshots. The writing was on the wall.

Securing an internship at a studio *before* leaving would have been a better strategic move. At least he could get face time with decision makers who could help his career.

Well, moving from one friend's couch to another got old real quick. The savings he had did run dry. And, the start-up magazine didn't get off the ground. My friend had to move back to Washington State a few months later.

So, why is it that people like James's dad, who came to America with thirty-five dollars in his pocket, are able to survive and raise their children? He took any jobs that would pay him money. Remember, James's dad had a comfortable life in Korea, but he knew that to make it in America, "beggars can't be choosers." My friend was too selective. And, this was not the time for cutting out options. He could've worked graveyard at McDonalds and chased his dreams during the day. But, he literally took the "follow your passion" mantra to the *nth* degree and thought he had to do it 24/7. You can, but you have to add common sense to make it work.

Have a Clear Plan

Unlike my friend who didn't have a clear plan to succeed, Teddy Zee, another Asian Hall of Fame honoree, has a totally different story. Teddy's is a name recognized in Hollywood because of his more than twenty-five years of experience in the field of entertainment. He's the executive producer behind blockbuster films like *Life or Something Like It* and *Pursuit of Happyness.* Born to Chinese immigrant parents, the New York native's childhood was far from the glitz and glamour of Hollywood.

His mom was a housewife who spoke limited English. This made communication with Teddy difficult during his formative years. His father worked in the kitchen of a hotel and never made more than $17,000 a year. "I saw how hard my dad struggled to make money. My takeaway was that I never wanted to work just to make money. I wanted to work and be fulfilled through my work."

During his childhood years, Teddy used watching TV and films as an escape, but recalls hardly seeing any Asians in the visual media. "I always felt a little alienated in the world."

He had a fascination with pop culture, TV, and film, and Teddy's first job out of college was in the human resources department for NBC. It was there that he studied the careers of people who work in the creative side at the networks and studios. "They helped shape what the public sees. One day, I asked the president of NBC programming how he got his job. Among the things he said was that he went to Harvard Business School. So, I applied there and got in."

Since the NBC executive gave Teddy a clear model on what he did to get the job he's doing today, Teddy followed his advice. He started applying for scholarships to help pay for his Ivy League education because he couldn't afford to pay his way and didn't mind the debt if it would get him what he needed to succeed.

When he graduated with his Harvard Business School degree, Teddy went back to that NBC executive and said, "Here I am with my

Harvard degree." The NBC executive then introduced him to some people in the industry, which led to Teddy's first executive position at Paramount studios. It came with his own parking spot with his name. But, it only paid him $30,000 a year. He knew, though, that with hard work, this was just a starting salary. At least he was finally doing a job that he had always wanted—he was the creative power behind the camera.

Within a few months, Teddy said, "My salary doubled, and doubled, and doubled, but even at $30,000, I wasn't too bothered. I was doing a job that I loved." Two things helped Teddy gauge that he was on the right career path and his time was well spent. 1) He loved coming to work. 2) He was getting paid well to do it and the quality of his life wasn't suffering. As an added bonus, Teddy gets to watch TV and films as part of the job. He's immersed in pop culture, magazines, and entertainment. When he posts his status updates and pictures on Facebook, it's all tied to his work. His work is his life. "The lines are clearly blurred because I love what I do. My community work, my social life, and my professional work all mix together."

Don't Get Distracted

During his childhood, Teddy used entertainment as a way to escape his reality. He's not alone. Many of us do it, including me. But, it only becomes a problem if it gets in the way of your dream. Do you spend more of your time on activities that distract from your goals, like watching too much TV or surfing the web? As you know, time is our most precious commodity. Once it's gone, it's gone. You can't take it back. As I reflect back on my formative years, I realize that I wasted so much time. For one, I spent a lot of my time in front of the television set. Granted, I used the medium to learn how to speak English. But, there were times I watched TV while I did my homework. Now, looking back, it wasn't the most productive use of my time because I would go over the same math problem for hours.

On top of that, I often spent my evenings in grade school at home with TV as my babysitter, or reading a book. My parents' funds were limited, so I couldn't take piano lessons or do sports. Yes, TV kept me out of trouble, but it became my main source of entertainment. I should've been outside playing with my friends and developing myself socially.

When I entered high school, I had more freedom, as my parents weren't so strict and I didn't need to come home right after school all the time. If they had adopted a strict parenting style, they may have set back or damaged my future prospects. As I was the first in my immigrant family with ambitions for higher education, my mom understood that I needed to be a well-rounded student with extracurricular activities—that was critical to me getting into college.

While I was in high school, I was able to do so much. When you take TV watching out of the equation, I had the free time to do other activities. I was taking honors classes, learning how to drive, being a cheerleader, volunteering for humanitarian causes, and working, too. When I was a restaurant busser, a conversation with a customer changed my way of thinking. He asked me, "What do you want to be when you get older?"

After being interviewed for the Federal Way (Washington) newspaper when I was Miss Federal Way, I shared with the customer, "I want to be a storyteller."

He said, "In order to be successful at it, you must do it every day." I processed what my customer said, and began to understand the depth and context of what he was saying. Success wasn't going to happen overnight for me, just like I later learned from Richard Cho's story. I had to submerge myself in activities that were going to develop me as a storyteller. Since I was passionate about storytelling, reading, and daily writing, those needed to be part of my regular routine.

With my days filled with productive activities instead of distractions, my grades didn't suffer. They got better. Each activity fed another aspect of my life that would help me get closer to being a storyteller. Instead of watching TV, I used that time to practice my next debate speech, or I used that time to concentrate on my homework because I had a game to attend the next day. Instead of watching sitcoms on TV, I used that time to read a newspaper. I didn't just read it for information, but I broke it down on how the reporter crafted his or her story.

When I'd be tempted by "distractions," it was pretty easy to say no. There was too much to do that day. With this laser-focused attitude, I graduated in the top 10 percent of my class of more than 350 students.

That type of work ethic carried through my college years where I was juggling three jobs, a full class load, and producing the student-run campus TV station.

And, this discipline became a prevalent aspect of my adult life. When I was a TV reporter, I would watch the TV news, as it was part of the job. However, I did allow myself some wiggle room with one guilty pleasure—watching one reality show for that season. But, otherwise, I felt no need to indulge myself.

When I left the news business, I no longer had any use for TV. And, I dropped my cable subscription completely in my late twenties and early thirties. When I did have the itch to watch a show, I would go to the gym and watch it on a treadmill. As a result, I got into the best shape of my life.

Today, there are more distractions than just TV. Facebook and other social networking sites can be time wasters. If your job is in the media like Teddy's or mine, then you need to keep up on these platforms. But, if you find yourself posting your life on Facebook, spending hours surfing the net, neglecting your workout, not eating healthy, not doing your day job or working on your real goals, then that's when a little entertainment now and then becomes a "paralyzing distraction."

I've shared this story because I ask you to make an honest assessment of yourself. How well are you managing your time? If it's not well, seriously, what are you waiting for? You don't have much time.

Honey-Do List

You've heard of the term "honey-do list," which is a list of activities you give a partner to do. Now, let's turn that "honey-do list" to "Honey . . . this is *your* to-do list." Let's go back to goal setting. Ask yourself, "What do I want to do?" Richard Cho wanted to be an executive of a major sports franchise. Through research, he realized he had to get further education. Teddy Zee simply asked his boss to define his career path to success, and he followed it to the "T."

When you write down your goal, post that goal everywhere—on your computer, your bathroom mirror, or in your journal. This becomes a constant reminder to make your long-term goal much more prevalent in your daily life. You've heard the phrase: out of mind, out of sight. Well, it works the other way as well: in your sight, in your mind.

Now, break down that goal. If it's to buy a house, you may need to save a certain amount of money. If it's to get promoted in your company, find out from your boss the skills he or she used to move up the ladder. If it's to get a job, it's as simple as applying. When I was laid off as a TV reporter, I spent my time sending out résumé tapes, e-mailing news directors, and talking to others in the business and getting my name out there.

Nothing worthwhile comes easily, and there are no overnight successes.

In summary, we are all given twenty-four hours a day—the rich, the poor, the immigrants, and the native-born. Those who succeed are just better with their use of time than others, and those who don't get caught up in distractions. Which category do you fall in?

CHAPTER SEVEN

Find Your Passion

What makes you want to get up in the morning? I ask that because I find people who are living their passion can't wait to start their day, as opposed to hitting the "snooze" button and getting a few more minutes of sleep. They live life with conviction. They walk with purpose. They have a "can do" attitude.

I like to look at passion as one's dreams. Dreams come in all sizes, and their fulfillment can come at all levels. Some people take on humbling jobs like housekeeping to fund their children's higher education. Some actresses will work as nannies or actors as cab drivers for years just to be available for a big part on television or in film; others work a real job, support a family, and use their "acting" skills at the Little Theater on the weekends. I loved being a TV reporter, but now I use that "presence" to talk to groups of young professionals and immigrants on how to improve their lives. So, what is your passion?

Nailing Your Passion

And if you don't know your passion, it's okay. It's a feeling of excitement that comes when we least expect it, and it can change or evolve. If you are not 100 percent sure what your passion is, sometimes a question like, "How do I want my energy and time spent?" can help nail it for you. That's a question a former Starbucks executive, Jane Park, asked herself when she was trying to figure out what would stir her passion for the rest of her working life. Being her own boss appealed to her, but that would mean leaving corporate America. Jane admits that it wasn't something she imagined in her future. "No. I had no idea," she told me with a laugh. "I'm not a serial entrepreneur."

Today, Jane has a growing nail parlor business and is recognized by the national media as a beauty expert. She came up with the concept while attending a corporate event at Starbucks that centered on sports. This made Jane ask herself a question: "What happens if you're not a huge sports fan? Are there activities that build morale in a setting that's geared more toward women, like salons and spas?" Jane found plenty of such retreats for women, but their accommodations were minimal, and the socializing aspect was dampened because quieter "spa voices" were encouraged. That's when an idea was sparked in Jane's mind—to create a nail salon where customers can socialize and have fun. At Julep Nail Parlor, you get what you pay for in more ways than one. "The cost of a pedicure at Julep is much higher, and it's because of all the things that we're doing to create a good environment that doesn't exploit female workers or customers."

You won't find carcinogens in the products or toxic fumes in the air at Julep. The tools used at her parlor are sterilized in the same way as those used by dentists and doctors. In addition, its workers have access to healthcare benefits. "We have a true commitment to improving and empowering women."

But it took Jane a long time to listen to her inner voice and follow her passion. Leaving Starbucks as an executive wasn't something her immigrant parents initially supported, especially leaving to open a nail salon, of all businesses.

"There's something about being a child of an immigrant where you are supposed to be responsible for your parents' hopes and dreams. They've given up so much for you in a way that's different than when your kids are already growing up in American society."

Choose Your Passion, Not What Others Want for You

Jane has struggled to find the balance between pleasing her parents and pleasing herself. Her parents emigrated from South Korea to Toronto, Canada, when Jane was just four years old. "They always found apartments next door to libraries when I was growing up. So, they were really encouraging me to spend time there. I think they actually used the library as a babysitter, frankly."

Growing up, Jane remembers an atmosphere where her parents expected a lot from her. "If I brought home a test that I had gotten a 99 on, the first statement was always, 'What happened to the (other) 1 percent?'"

After high school, Jane knew that college was certainly in her future. The University of Toronto was a likely choice because her parents thought it was the best university in Canada. Jane had her eyes set on Princeton, but not for the reasons one would think. "It was an attempt to gain some independence and have a real college experience, and not have to live at home while going to college."

Jane was accepted into Princeton and majored in public policy. After college, she wanted to go to India with her professor to work for a nonprofit organization that gave micro-financing loans to women to help fund their projects. "But, I knew my parents would never be excited about that."

As a daughter who always wanted to please her parents, Jane applied to Yale Law School to assure them India was just a one-year stint, not a long-term decision. "But, when I told them my plan, they both broke down crying. I had never seen my dad cry before. So, I went to law school. I got guilted into this decision, which was never the plan. It was supposed to be the excuse to do my India project."

After law school, Jane worked as a consultant and eventually was hired as an executive at Starbucks. She worked as a director of new ventures, looking for different growth opportunities for the company.

Then she left Starbucks to start her own venture. What do her parents have to say now that Jane is a successful entrepreneur? She said they're supportive, but it helps that she's also the mother of two children. "When it comes to their grandkids, they can do anything," she said with a laugh. "And, it's okay. They're wonderful. Oh, 'What a good job you did!'"

In the end, when Jane followed her passion and succeeded, her parents came around. She gives this advice to anyone who wants to follow his or her passion—good is the new perfect. "It's really hard to let go of the idea that everything has to be perfect. When you are starting something new, there are so many things going on, especially for those with a family and kids. You're juggling a lot. And women put a lot of pressure on themselves to be perfect in a lot of dimensions. I think as a generation we have to let that go."

Expect No Entitlement

She adds that following your passion is a marathon, and things won't always go your way. "The most important thing that you can be doing is making mistakes and learning from them." Jane said it's also healthy to be able to have a good sense of humor. You'll need it because you'll have to work hard and put in long hours. If you are starting your own business, it may mean doing grunt work, including emptying the trash.

Despite the obstacles immigrants face, from language barriers to financing to a slew of other problems, many find ways to be successful. You've read stories about Jane Park, James Sun, Thach Nguyen,

Richard Cho, and many other immigrants who became successful as entrepreneurs or in their respective fields, and in some cases made history. How did they find a way to live their passion despite coming from extremely humble beginnings? According to Marcia Drew Hohn, the director of the Public Education Institute for The Immigrant Learning Center, "Immigrants expect to work hard and have no sense of entitlement." They come here with nothing. And, they hunger for all the opportunity. Just being in this country is an opportunity in and of itself. The pursuit of happiness is a choice and not an entitlement.

Entitlement Leads to Disappointment

Dee Wallace, star of *E.T.: The Extra-Terrestrial* and the author of *Bright Light,* said working in that film was life changing, especially for a girl from Kansas City who had only been in Hollywood for a few years. "I loved the role. I loved the film. I loved what the film did for the world and what it is still doing for the world. It's an enigma or a duality of life, when you are so proud of what you did. You had so much joy in it, and you expect it to go on forever, and it doesn't."

Things turned sour for Dee when she fell into the trap of entitlement. She expected the major blockbuster film and working with Steven Spielberg to catapult her into a lot of mainstream films. "It just didn't happen. And little by little, I lost my light. I lost belief in myself. I started blaming the world. I started blaming God. I became my own creator of the opposite thing of what I wanted. I fell out of the joy. I went into fear. I went into anger. You literally become your own cancer-creator in your life without knowing it."

Dee fell into a depression when the studios didn't call. She was counting on the work as an outlet for her creativity. She admits she lives and breathes to have the ability to create. "When that's taken away from us, we're hit with kind of a triple-edge sword. You're desperately unhappy and depressed because you have no creative outlet for this amazing energy that you need to create with."

Just as quickly as Dee let herself head into a downward spiral, she realized it was within her control to turn things around. It began with her and so she could do something about it. And, she encourages those who are in a similar situation to turn it around, she said. It begins with us; we have to stop "blaming God, the world, and other people." She said that self-reflection is critical, with questions like, "How bright can I shine my light?" "What makes me happy?" "What's going to bring my passion back to me?"

Dee focused on her talent to create. She ended up teaching acting classes, which renewed her love of acting, and she started doing more television later in her career, to great success. She's also a published author. Dee realized that entitlement leads to disappointment. Instead, ask the question: what can I do to . . .

Fill that Void

I can relate to what Dee was feeling when she stopped creating for herself. She let others control her destiny, expecting the phone to ring off the hook with more starring roles after *E.T.: The Extra-Terrestrial.* When the waiting game went on and on, she felt a void because she wasn't creating. When I left TV news after five years of reporting and anchoring, I had no idea how much I would miss storytelling. This also came at a time when a marriage engagement didn't work out. Not only did I have a professional void, but I had a personal one too.

While leaving the news business was my decision, I did miss interviewing people and cultivating stories. I left to work at a successful start-up company as an account executive, with a promotion to sales manager soon after. But, it didn't fill the void. Sales work is a numbers game. The more people you call, the more the potential revenue. My day became similar to the film *Groundhog Day*. And, I felt something was missing in my life.

As a way to heal from a broken engagement, I started journal writing my thoughts and feelings. It hit me just how much I missed storytelling. I was doing a sales job that provided the financial rewards that I needed during that time in my life, but I still needed to write or create. I learned that the creative process, like Dee discovered, could include more than a one-size-fits-all solution. I found my creative outlet by acting in commercials, emceeing or hosting events, and writing for numerous publications. And, this book has certainly allowed my creative side to shine by interviewing people and sharing their stories. As a result, I became a happier and more fulfilled person. I realized that I was responsible for filling that void since I removed the creative outlet myself. What void do you have in your life?

Feed Your Passion

One of my best friends from childhood, Catherine, loves to cook. Her passion is food. While she doesn't own her own restaurant *yet,* she feeds her passion regularly by catering extravagant meals for her friends or watching and learning from more experienced chefs. I have been fortunate to try many of her dishes. She now works at a restaurant owned by Tom Douglas, an American chef who authored several cookbooks and appeared in a reality show, *Iron Chef*. Catherine also enjoys eating at restaurants that serve foods that taste and look like works of art. Food is her life.

She appreciates food so much that she even backpacked across Italy, eating and journaling about her food experience. What kind of olive oil is good with certain dishes? How do you make authentic pizza, unlike what you find at fast food restaurants? She didn't share her entries with the world; she did the trip for herself to nourish her body, mind, and soul. She also went to culinary school there to hone her skills. Again, she followed her passion and created a road map to make food a regular part of her life because it brought her so much joy. Again, I'm not talking about food as only nourishment, but food as a passion and an expression of one's aesthetic sense.

When Catherine returned to Washington State from Italy, she felt revived and ready to experiment with her findings in the kitchen. When we lived together, I was the fortunate guinea pig. She introduced me to authentic Bolognese sauce and truffles.

This passion for food isn't some grandiose ambition or huge financial burden on her, but it sure brings her joy that's priceless. If the restaurant happens or not, at least she won't have a hole in her heart, because she continues to feed her passion regularly. Catherine realizes she is responsible for her happiness, and that happiness is to feed her passion.

Help Others

Your passion may be to help others. Is it volunteer work? Is it to sit on the board of a nonprofit organization? Perhaps it's to run for public office. Raj Goyle has a passion for helping others. "From a very young age, I was interested in public service, and I very much believe in giving back to the community."

With a desire to make a difference in his community, Raj decided to run for office in 2006. Raised in Wichita, Kansas, the largest city in the state, Raj thought he'd be a great advocate for his community. "I felt a real need to actually step forward and run for office because I saw that the representative in my home district wasn't really representing mainstream values, and was voting against public education, being anti-immigrant, and not listening to people with a different party label. I thought my values were more representative of the district."

And, the voters agreed. Raj won his seat in the Kansas State House of Representatives, despite the fact that at the time, there were only ten Indian Americans living in his district that had a total population of more than 20,000 people.

"Before I ran for office in 2006, no Indian American or Asian American had run for or won an election in the state of Kansas."

While Raj made history, he felt that his position made a bigger impact on the political landscape statewide and encouraged immigrants and Asian Americans to consider a life of public service. As an elected member of the House of Representatives in a state with 2.5 million people and a budget of $13 billion, Raj says there was certainly a level of intrigue about him at the capitol as the first Asian American to hold public office in the state at that time. "My cultural background . . . shapes who I am from the way I look to what's in my head, to what's in my heart and to what my values are. I had an experience where my parents were Indian Americans [and] proud of their heritage in an area that didn't have a tremendous amount of ethnic diversity."

While he's no longer serving in the legislature, as he lost an aggressive campaign for the US House in 2010, Raj said the culture of the House of Representatives and the political system will never be the same because now an Asian American has broken the barrier and forged a pathway for others to come behind him.

Today, Raj continues to pursue his passion. He is giving to others through philanthropic endeavors. Will he run again for office? "Public service is in my blood."

Give Back to Organizations that Align with Your Values

Like Raj, I also enjoy giving back to the community. As I am writing this book, I sit on three boards: Ascend, the *International Examiner,* and Stiletto Woman in Business Awards. It's a good feeling to share my time and know that peoples' lives are being enriched by my involvement with these organizations. While they require a lot of time, I feel like it's a mutually beneficial relationship because my mind and soul are being fed, too.

Ascend is a nonprofit organization that reaches 15,000 people across the country. Its focus is to nurture today's Pan Asian American leaders as well as those of tomorrow. It's been hard all my life to find mentors from my background. This is an organization where I can be mentored by people who may have had some of the same struggles, such as learning how to speak a foreign language and assimilating into a new country. There's that unspoken connection and an instant bond formed when you meet a fellow emigrant from the same country or region who also came from humble beginnings.

When I was the events chair for the Seattle Ascend chapter, I have brought in big-name speakers whose stories have been featured in this book, like Dr. Connie Mariano and James Sun.

By bringing in these high-profile names to talk to the members of the organization, I want both young and seasoned professionals to listen to people who are the best in their fields. This way, their minds are being injected with passion and insight that will help them in their careers.

I know my time is well-spent on Ascend when I hear stories like Nath Lam's. Nathan is a student member who received ten job offers before graduating.

"They [Ascend events] provided top-tier insight on how to progress from a student's standpoint and have the world perceive me as I wished. Not only professionally, but on a personal one-on-one basis as well. It made me want to create an image of myself that I wanted others to recognize as me," said Nathan.

Comments like this show that my efforts are shaping the careers of many Asian American professionals. I can't help but feel good. Remember, passion is a feeling.

The *International Examiner* (*IE*) is the oldest nonprofit Pan Asian American media in the country. As you know, many newspapers are challenged to generate revenue in a dying medium, and the *IE* is no different. As the co-vice president of this nonprofit organization, I contribute ideas on how to use our website as a main source for its readership and revenue. It's no easy task.

But why would I devote so much time to an organization that faces so many challenges? Is this good use of my time? My "day job," helping board-certified doctors with their online presentations, is already demanding. Why add more to my already full plate? It's because I believe in the content of the paper. I feel like my expertise can help the paper transition into the modern media, especially since immigration is a hot topic today, and immigrant stories are something that the paper covers. It gives a voice to Pan Asian immigrants who are underrepresented in the mainstream media. Those are two things that I am passionate about. I am an immigrant, and rarely do I come across information or stories that I connect with immediately.

Finally, I make time to sit on the advisory board of Stiletto Woman in Business Awards because it helps empower women. I'm surrounded by women who have unique stories. They run successful companies or are respected in their industries. And, the synergy from our conference calls is invaluable and nourishes my mental health.

That's why I say it's critical to choose to spend your time on projects that align with your values and beliefs. Otherwise, your volunteer work may feel more like work than passion.

Passion Is an Attitude

I've shared with you that passion is a feeling, but it's also an attitude. I met Anna Mok, a partner at Deloitte, a global consulting firm in New York City, when Hurricane Irene forced the cancellation of the Ascend National Convention in August 2011. We had a lot of downtime, and I found out more about Anna, who also sits on the national Ascend board.

This immigrant from Hong Kong was raised in San Francisco and went to college at the University of California, Berkeley. She majored in finance and business. But don't think she's just about numbers or math. "I was always good at math, but was never passionate about it."

Yet, Anna has a passion for challenging herself and stimulating her mind. That's what drew her to Deloitte, where she started in the audit practice. "What we look for at Deloitte are people who are great critical thinkers, have good judgment, and can really connect with people and create trust," said Anna.

Because Anna found an environment that allowed her to problem-solve, she wasn't a clock puncher or working a nine-to-five schedule. She did her job well, staying long hours and focusing on making an impact in her job. With high aspirations to be a leader within the organization, Anna looked within herself to what she could contribute to the company—and that was her passion. Twenty years later, she is a successful partner with the firm.

Beyond her job, Anna also has a passionate attitude about life from her community involvement with Ascend as well as from her personal endeavors. "I try something new every year, but I'm not that disciplined." Yet she enjoys the physical challenge and mental commitment. This mom, whose daughter is eleven years old at the time of this interview, recently finished her first half-marathon. "I am not a runner. I hate running, in fact." And she became certified as a scuba diver even though she's not a big beachgoer.

"Those kinds of things are important to do just for yourself, because they give you different ways to celebrate your own accomplishments and not just hear a boss or your company tell you what success should look like."

Better Yourself

Like Anna, your passion could simply be to better yourself. My former roommate, Shanell, shared with me that her passion is to just have a good life. She's already unique in her immediate family by not relying on any government assistance and being self-sufficient. "When I'm old and gray and everything is falling apart, I can say I had a really good run. I fulfilled everything I set out to do." Her desire for an improved life includes meeting new people, having a better understanding of how the world works, and improving herself. Shanell's desire to seek a better life stems from her childhood. She was born in Los Angeles, California, and raised all over the country, including Seattle, Washington, and Providence, Rhode Island. She remembers her childhood as a time she moved from one project to the next. "You have your homeless, ghetto girls who can't formulate an English sentence, and then the wannabe thugs." That environment, she said, taught her to be independent and self-sufficient. Before she was a teenager, she witnessed young girls having babies in order to get government assistance. That's when Shanell realized that was not the life for her and promised herself to do whatever she could to ensure she doesn't become another statistic.

In her mid-twenties, Shanell saved up enough money for a one-way airplane ticket to leave that environment and moved to Issaquah, Washington, to live with relatives. The twenty-seven-year-old, who had never left her immediate family, got the courage to start a new chapter out west. "The East Coast wasn't doing anything for me. I needed a change: new scenery, another location, and different people." Shanell remembers being scared as she landed at Sea-Tac International Airport; however, she also recalls breathing freely for the first time in years. "I knew life would get better. A clean slate."

As soon as she moved in with her relatives, Shanell immediately got acclimated to her new life and started job hunting. Within a month, she started working at a retail store to save up money so she could live on her own. She had no car, and walked fifteen minutes to work with each way. But, each step she took, Shanell knew she was headed in the right direction. "Each day is a success for me because I'm going a lot farther than I thought I would. I'm doing this on my own."

Shanell lives in her own apartment with friends. She works in childcare but didn't realize her love for children until recently. The determination to have a better life has motivated her to take a two-hour bus commute to work. When we lived together, I heard Shanell wake-up at 4:00 A.M. to start her day and get ready for work; she's an inspiration to me. Shanell sees this job as an opportunity. "I am not a victim. I am in control of my own destiny." This young woman moving forward with her life should encourage those who also feel trapped in their environment to make a change. They can find their passion in life just like she has and move forward with it.

Lacks Passion

I have another friend with so much God-given talent, yet I see that his life has no passion. He lives a minimalist life of contentment. I see nothing wrong with being content, but imagine living life with enthusiasm versus just coasting by as a window shopper.

My friend's house is almost paid off; he lives within his means, and because of an inheritance, he has never had to work a tasking job. He does write a little. Life is comfortable for my friend.

I can often find him spending time alone rather than being out there creating, networking, and finding synergy. He's all about being content. No big risks. No disruptions in his routine life. He doesn't have high days or low days. His day-to-day life lacks variety and excitement.

When I asked him, "What's your passion," he couldn't tell me. Nothing makes him want to get out of bed and start creating something new. He doesn't get involved in community activities where he could share his wisdom and talent with others. Granted, he does write articles and so he is sharing his wisdom with his readers. But, most of the things he does lack any real "oomph."

While he has more material comforts than Shanell, who is working on being an independent woman, which life would you prefer? One of contentment with all of the material things of a good life? Or, one in which you live your life with purpose and you're on the way to creating a better life for yourself?

This all reminds me of someone who told me that one of his favorite movies is *Serendipity*, where at the end the John Cusack character follows his passion for a woman he only met once in his life but has sought out for years. He realizes on the eve of his marriage to his current girlfriend that he can't marry her because she's not his soul mate. His friend, who writes obituaries for *The New York Times*, is inspired by his quest and tells him, "You know, the Greeks didn't write obituaries, they only asked one question after a man died: 'Did he have passion?'"

Passion is an emotion. Right now, what is your emotion regarding your life? Passionate? Passionless?

CHAPTER EIGHT

Physical and Mental Health 101

Many immigrants learn to become totally self-sufficient, but it's okay sometimes to ask for help. I had a lot of stress in my life late in 2011 from my grandma passing away and a relationship issue that wasn't going so well, to the point of losing weight and feeling generally distraught. I was in a funk. I tried to get along on my own with the help of my friends and family and kept myself busy with activities I enjoyed, but when I still couldn't sleep or even eat well, I realized that I needed professional help. There were issues that I had simply shelved over the years that now resurfaced. It was time I battled those demons.

I find that my mental health and physical well-being aren't separate entities, but blend together as one. And, when they become separated, either my mind or body will let me know that they are not working in harmony.

When my mind is troubled, my body speaks to me by becoming more tired and sensitive, and therefore, I'm more likely to get sick. And, when my body isn't at its best, I get headaches and become irritable or depressed. I also don't eat as well. I grab anything in front of me, which are usually snacks like cookies and chocolates with very little nutritional value. I get this sugar high and then crash. It becomes a downward spiral. Soon, my mental and physical state affects the people around me. I then start feeling guilty and am hard on myself for falling short of people's expectations, and, even worse, from my expectations of how I want to interact with others. Being a busy and stubborn gal, I just keep pushing through the muck, often ignoring what my mind and body are telling me—that I need to take care of me first.

Interestingly enough, while I was going through this slump, my work didn't suffer nor did my contribution to the nonprofit boards that I sit on. In fact, I was breaking company records and getting praised for my volunteer efforts as this turmoil unfolded. So, I told myself that I'm in control and everything is okay since others see my performance as effective. But, I knew deep down that something wasn't right when I felt so emotionally depleted. My mood didn't match my performance. That's when I crashed hard. Soon, years of ignoring what my mind and body had been saying, "Take care of Maureen first," ended up with me in a counseling session and talking about old wounds. My advice is not to let it get to that point. This is why it's important to:

Take Care of Yourself Now

If you don't, it will catch up to you in one way or another. So, a day at the spa or at a nail parlor or lunch with girlfriends; or for you guys, taking in a basketball game or exercise; or for both genders, reading a good book or more family time or even just a few more hours of sleep can recharge your batteries regularly. I have learned to do this frequently as these activities feed into my happiness—I just forget sometimes. When I'm a "happy Maureen," not only does everyone in my environment benefit, but I also feel better about myself. (Note to self: take my own advice more often.)

I got a wake-up call recently about being human and mortal when my grandmother had an unexpected stroke, leaving half her body paralyzed. I watched this independent woman who survived the Great Depression and buried her husband and son—a widow for thirty years—now become dependent on machines to feed and hydrate her body and on nurses and doctors to give her 24/7 care. It was a shock seeing her like this and remembering Grandma Mary's active lifestyle with her social calendar filled with church friends and square dancing. But, during the latter part of her life, I watched her lack of motivation take its toll because of her declining health, which decreased my Grandma's active lifestyle. Those were things that were feeding her mind, body, and soul. Could she have worked out more? Yes. Could she have eaten healthier? Yes. Could she [fill in the blank]? Yes. When this stroke happened, it shook me and reminded me of the importance of always taking care of ourselves first. Our health is something that we should never take for granted.

Two weeks after Grandma's stroke, she passed away, just a week after Thanksgiving. I'm thankful to have spent one more holiday with her. Despite her having lived a full life, I still wasn't prepared for her death. I thought I had a few more holidays with her. I hoped she'd witness a few more milestones in my life, from my wedding to the birth of my first child, but nothing is set in stone. This wasn't God's plan. She was eighty-six years old.

Life is Short

Grandma Mary is a family member, along with my mother, whose life I have shared the longest. Her death made me analyze my own life. Am I living the life I have always wanted? Am I surrounding myself with activities and people that fulfill me? Am I happy? Do I have any regret with the choices I've made? After all, life is short. After my time of self-reflection, I can proudly say that I have lived with very *few* regrets. I say few because earlier in my life, I wish I had made a few better choices. In some cases, I wish I had had more courage.

This reminds me of Maria Castañón Moats, who is the chief diversity officer and an assurance partner with PricewaterhouseCoopers LLP (PwC). I listened to her story when she was the keynote speaker at the Ascend National Convention at which I was the co-emcee. Here's her story:

> I'm a first generation Mexican American, and my first language was Spanish. Family is very important to me. I have two children, three siblings, fourteen aunts and uncles, over forty first cousins, and too many second cousins to keep track. We're still close, even though we live in different states.
>
> While my family always encouraged me to succeed, they also wanted to shelter me from the unknown. Mexican culture tends to be very protective of women. This cultural push and pull—between safety and risk taking—was challenging for me. For example, I was the first member of my family to go to college. My parents were very proud and believed in my ability to achieve this milestone. But I agreed to go to the local university in my own hometown to stay close to home. At the time, the trade-off was worth it: I could rely on the safety and security of my family while pursuing my education. However, I do wonder what might have happened if I had had the courage to venture farther from home.
>
> Risk-taking might not always feel comfortable, but I believe it's essential for career growth and development. Two years ago, I was asked to move to the East Coast to take on a challenging role. I was really comfortable in my market. I was surrounded by family and friends. I was a successful client service partner; I understood my role and how I fit into that office. Yet here was a chance to see how the firm operated on a national level. This move would give me exposure to PwC leaders and influential

> partners. If I wanted to advance to the next level in my career, this was exactly what I needed.
>
> Unlike college, the time was right—the stakes were higher, and I had courage. I was on a journey, and although I didn't know exactly where this move might take me, I knew it was a risk worth taking. I advise my protégés to run toward challenges and embrace the unknown. But being open to opportunities doesn't mean just accepting them on their own terms. We must constantly negotiate between cultures—for me, that means staying true to my Mexican heritage and taking risks to be a pioneer at PwC.

I agree with Maria, as I've taken some huge risks in my own life professionally and personally. I moved to Savannah, Georgia, a city where I knew no one, to pursue a career in TV news. I needed to prove to myself that I was a lot stronger than I thought at the time. I was excited and terrified at the same time. Like Maria, I made the move when it was right for me. And, it was good for my mental health. Maria is definitely a role model for other Hispanics in corporate America.

Maria wouldn't be where she is today if it weren't for courage.

Think Before You Act

While Maria still wonders what might have happened had she chosen to go to that other college, I do admire her for choosing her local university. She didn't base her decision entirely on emotions, but analyzed the situation. She thought before she acted. David Van Maren, who was an orphan near the border of North and South Korea, lived in an atmosphere of hunger and disease as well as not knowing what love was. He's currently the state director and producer of Miss Washington USA, Miss Washington Teen USA, Miss Idaho USA, and Miss Idaho Teen USA, all of which are operated by the Miss Universe Organization, a joint partnership with Donald J. Trump and NBCUniversal. David is also the cofounder of MRKd.tv, an online entertainment and merchandising network and platform. He mentors young people on how to think before you act, something he said he didn't always do when he was a child or teen, and was often picked on at school for looking different from his Anglo parents. David was adopted by a Dutch family who lived in Northeastern Oregon. Growing up, David had to deal with racial issues. "If you have a different look than others, then people will judge you based on your appearance. No matter what happens," David said.

David had to defend himself in fights regularly. It's something that he's not proud of and he didn't always think before he acted. "It says a lot about a person on how you react to a situation versus the action itself. So many times I didn't react the proper way. Even when people said things that were spiteful, I could've reacted differently, instead of always retaliating, which didn't help my situation."

As David reflects back on his younger years, he said it was tough for his Caucasian American adoptive family to understand the bullying taking place in his life. David admits he wasn't good at communicating and sharing his feelings with them about the constant torment at school. There were only a few kids there who really tried to understand his journey, and the lack of diversity in his community didn't help. So, David rebelled throughout his teenage years from all the hurt and anger that had built up. Rather than being seen as a victim, David was now seen as a troublemaker.

Tired of being picked on, he looked around and realized that the kids who excelled at school or sports tended to be treated differently. That's when David got involved in sports and began developing a better attitude. By his senior year, the fights at school stopped. David learned a valuable lesson when he put his energy toward bettering himself. "If you're good in school and/or sports, you start becoming more accepted, and so that was one of the biggest reasons why I took up sports, because I was tired of being the brunt of the jokes, racial comments, and physical attacks."

After high school, David continued to wrestle in college. During college, he was exposed to greater ethnic diversity and even dated a Korean girl at one point. Fitness became a big part of David's life, and he became a fitness trainer during and after college. On the side, he also started doing some extra work in films, mainly because of his physique. That's when he met a casting director who eventually became his mentor in the world of show business. That life-changing relationship forged a lasting career, and David is now in the entertainment industry and at one point was the owner of a model/talent/sports agency.

Today, he works with young people through reality programming, pageants, modeling, and other entertainment-related fields. He shares his life story to help them have more social acumen to make smarter choices for themselves, advice he wished someone had given him back then.

Interestingly, I was introduced to David by one of his pageant contestants who I met for coffee. She needed some advice about breaking into the broadcasting industry, and she reached out to me since we had mutual friends. She then told me about David, and immediately I knew I had to meet this man since he seemed to be such a great mentor.

As I had breakfast with David and he told me his life story, I learned a lesson from him, one he instills in the lives of those around him: "Always take time or give yourself a moment to think before you react. Emotions come and go. Don't let what people say bother you. Don't let insignificant or unworthy things provoke you since you already have significance. It all comes down to you as a person and how far you want to go in life and what matters to you most. It all comes down to believing in the gifts you carry and having great faith."

Because as David remembers, when he thoughtlessly retaliated, it did nothing to improve his mental health.

What Matters to You Most?

Anna Mok, a partner at Deloitte, asks herself this question. *What makes me whole as a person?* "It's my family and friends, it's my community, and it's my professional life and my work." Anna said that these things play on her emotion and intellect; they define her as a person. That's what she focuses on to ensure she is mentally and physically healthy. "Devoting a lot of time to each of those [activities and people] doesn't feel like a burden because they energize me, and I get so much from them. I feel like I'm developing myself as a whole."

Anna says it helps that she's not one who needs a lot of alone time. "I'm very lucky I don't need a lot of downtime, so that gives me more time to do those things I love."

While it's good to have downtime and to be by yourself, complete isolation isn't healthy. Humans are designed to have relationships; we are social beings by nature. Through Anna's activities, she is developing personal and professional relationships essential for her growth as a person and to make her feel whole. The communities she created for herself are guiding her into being the woman she wants to be. But, she adds that relationships have to be permeable and not constraining to be healthy.

So, you may have to look at your life like a pie chart. What does your day-to-day look like? What makes you feel whole?

Your Pie Chart

People often tell me they cannot keep up with me, as I'm off from one project to the next. Why am I so busy and what am I busy doing? Like Anna, I'm doing projects that feed my soul. Each plays an important role in my life and they are all part of the "pie chart." I believe it's important to have a balanced life and not let one "slice" of my life consume me. When I'm doing projects and spending time with people who make me feel good, it makes me a *more* productive employee, one able to give *more* to others and do *more* in life.

Before I commit to a project or accept an invitation, I recently started asking myself this important question: what role does that activity or person fill in my life? With only twenty-four hours in a day to work with, I value my time regarding what I do and with whom I'm doing it as I don't want to spread myself too thin. These projects and the people I surround myself with are supposed to feed the soul and not tear it down.

Here's what my pie chart looks like. Being in a relationship carries the most weight in my life, followed by spending time with family and friends. Work and NW Productions, LLC projects (acting, writing, and contributing to news and casting calls for reality shows) are the next piece; and then exercising, volunteering, and attending retreats, and adventures (traveling and doing "first" experiences) fill up the rest of the pie chart. In addition, my faith is sprinkled throughout my pie chart.

Here's what I found that was insightful when I understood the "slices" in my pie chart and how they give me satisfaction. If I ever feel an emptiness or void, I can self-diagnose its source. Am I not exercising? Have I stopped traveling? Am I too buried in work and not spending time with people I enjoy? That way, I can start filling my pie chart with activities and people that make me smile.

I also encourage you to create your own pie chart. What do you like to do that gives you an extra bounce in your step? Who inspires you to live your best? Are you surrounding yourself with positive people? That way, you won't find yourself doing busy, unfulfilling work, but being busy doing what you love and feeling fulfilled.

Watch What You Eat

Since we are on the topic of "pie," I also ask you to look at how you feed your body. Many immigrants and those who come from humble beginnings (and even those with quite a bit of disposable income) fall into the trap of feeding their body with processed, fast foods.

I've seen immigrants who come to America and put on weight. There's a reason why this country is the most obese in the world: fast food, processed food, and frozen dinners are part of the American culture.

These same immigrants, who ate fresh food with lots of vegetables and fruits in their native country, find themselves consuming unhealthy meals here.

I introduced my former roommate Shanell to organic food, which she says was foreign to her while she lived in Rhode Island. I told her I pay more for the "organic" label, but I feel good that what I'm eating is not processed with preservatives that my body has a tough time flushing. And, now, I see Shanell pay a few more dollars to eat healthier. As a result, she dropped a few more pounds when she was living with me.

When I was going to college, I would eat four bagels a day and I put on some weight. I found them filling, especially for a busy person like me. Now, I did exercise, but the weight would not come off. The pounds kept packing on. Bagels aren't bad for you, but the portions for my body type were way off. I indulged. One bagel a day I think would've been fine. But four? Unless I was playing football, that was just too excessive.

That's because my calorie intake was always more than my ability to burn it off. The math is simple. Eat more than you burn off, you will gain weight. I'm no different.

I finally began to shed the pounds when I started reading health magazines and realized that healthy food like salads were actually not that good for me when I added lots of high-fat Ranch dressing. So, I consciously started reading the food labels and their ingredients. If there are processed ingredients in the food, I tell myself, "a moment on the lips is forever on the hips." That usually makes me want to pass on the indulgence. Over the years, I've actually trained my body to enjoy eating fresh, unprocessed meals. The discipline has paid off.

Today, I never deprive myself of anything. I eat desserts frequently, but I just do so in sane portions. And, I always carve time to work out, even on vacations. I make it part of my calendar. And, if I don't, my body really feels it. I actually feel more sluggish and irritable. So, I make no excuses. I just make working out part of my life.

When I went back to my ten-year high school reunion, I admit that it felt good when people said, "You look great, Maureen." The affirmation from others motivated me to continue working out and making healthy food choices.

Fifth Degree black belt Marcello Alonso from Brazil remembers coming to his new country and seeing how accessible cheap food on the go is. But, he didn't see any benefits . . . at least when it came to his body. "The first day [I am in America], I eat at a fast food restaurant twice. I got really sick." While he saved more money eating at this popular fast food chain, these types of food didn't sit well with his body. He quickly reverted back to eating home-cooked meals, even though it cost him more. Since he makes his living teaching martial arts, he can't afford to have his health suffer.

Unfortunately, I have seen too many of my immigrant relatives fall into the habit of substituting fast food for the home-cooked meals that they normally would eat in the Philippines. They look at the savings. But over time, they can see their waistlines growing. They are surprised to see the big portions doled out in this country, because in the Philippines restaurants serve very small portions.

Since some of them have two jobs, it's hard for them to make time for workouts. So, now they are more conscious of what they feed their bodies since they are having a tough time shedding those extra pounds.

Move On from Unhealthy Relationships

Another unwanted weight worth shedding is relationships that weigh you down and don't feed your soul.

I was in a personal relationship where I started losing my voice and losing sight of the person I wanted to be. Every opinion, every belief, every move was seen as being wrong by this person. I let this happen for years! Finally, I had had enough.

I had to remove myself and get far away from this person. It was particularly tough because I also cared for him very much. I filled the void left by this breakup with other positive relationships. I became reacquainted with old friends, made new friends, spent more time with my family and people who cared about my mental and physical health.

Sometimes, there are relationships that just run their course.

As the first woman to head the White House Medical Unit, Dr. Connie Mariano worked with three presidents – George H. W. Bush, Bill Clinton, and George W. Bush. I heard this immigrant from the Philippines speak to an audience ranging from college students to CEOs about how she broke many barriers, such as being the first military woman to become a White House physician and the highest-ranking Filipino officer in naval history. She also spoke about her personal life.

When she was initially asked to join a list of candidates vying for the job of navy doctor to the White House, Mariano says, "I called my husband, Richard, at his law firm. I told him, and the first thing out of his mouth was 'Are you crazy?'" Her husband advised her to decline the job offer.

Dr. Mariano said, "I called him back, and he said 'You know what, on second thought, you have nothing to lose. You'll never get this job anyway.'"

She did get the job in June 1992. She served nine years at the White House, but her devotion to caring for the president and first family and going on over 130 overseas trips hurt her first marriage, which ended in divorce.

When I had lunch with her in Scottsdale, Arizona, she shared with me that there are people you grow up with and there are others you grow old with. She was able to diagnose this problem when the relationship with her high school sweetheart ran its course. You live and learn, and you move on.

Today, I'm happy to say, Dr. Mariano is remarried, and she found someone who complements her tenacity to live life.

She told me, you should be with someone who makes you a better person, and not someone who doesn't believe in you or your ambitions for yourself.

I had another friend who separated from a husband with an alcohol problem. She said that her husband's addiction to alcohol led to him lying all the time and being destructive. She could no longer live in peace with what her husband might or might not be doing. So, she got the courage to separate from him, and he sought help. She did it for herself and her one-year old son. My friend told me that if she stayed in the relationship as such, she was enabling him to drink. Her request for a separation made her husband realize that his addiction was taking its toll on his family and he might lose them. He is now receiving regular counseling.

Look at the people in your life. Are they also living a healthy life? Or, is it time to make some tough choices for the sake of your overall health?

Mental and Physical Health Begin with You

You may not have the training to diagnose your mental and physical health and know what is needed like Dr. Mariano, or the courage to leave an unhealthy relationship like my friend, but remember that your health begins with you. You have to figure out how to take better care of yourself, because in the end, it's your responsibility. If you surround yourself with people who care about you, they can offer guidance. But they can't make you improve your mental and physical health. It's all you.

Being healthy goes beyond eating properly and exercising weekly. I also don't smoke or drink or indulge in unhealthy habits like gambling. Eventually an unhealthy body will lead to an unhealthy mind.

A friend of mine, Julie Pham, became co-owner of her family's newspaper, *Người Việt Tây Bắc*. She told me that overall, being healthy means following your heart, listening to your voice, and doing what feels right no matter what stage of life. "I had just finished my PhD in history at Cambridge University. I knew in my heart I didn't want to stay in academia, and I wanted to try my hand at business. I also knew my parents were getting older and could use my help. Earnings from the newspaper fed my family for many years, and it put me through college. I felt it was right to return home and help."

To give you some context, let me share Julie's history. She was born in Cu Chi, a district outside Saigon famous for the "Cu Chi tunnels," which the Viet Cong guerillas used for hiding during the war. Julie's father had been a press officer in the South Vietnamese Navy. When the war ended in 1975, he was sentenced to three years of re-education camp. "I was born at the end of 1978. I was two months old when my father decided we would need to escape Vietnam. He feared having to go back to re-education camp. My parents were the first on both sides of their family to take that risk. We left by boat and stayed in a refugee camp in Indonesia for five months before finally making it over to the US."

Seattle became their home. The oldest child in the family, Julie grew up taking care of her two brothers while her parents were at work. "In Asian families, it's important for the oldest sibling to take care of his or her younger siblings. I remember having the most fun when we were very young and still living in public housing in Auburn, Washington. We invented games and created our own imaginary world. I was the ringleader. Other kids in the neighborhood joined."

Often, Julie and her siblings were also found playing at the newspaper's office, which became their second home.

Her dad started the business in the early 1980s after leaving the marine architect business. "He was tired of working for other people," Julie remembers. "My parents dreamed of owning their own business. Around the same time, the Vietnamese community was growing rapidly and there was a need for a newspaper to connect the community. *Nguòi Viêt Daily*, the largest Vietnamese language newspaper outside Vietnam, was established in Orange County in 1978. Vietnamese from all over the country subscribed to the newspaper. My mom said, "This is a good newspaper, why don't we bring it up here?" So, my parents started an independent branch of *Nguòi Viêt* in Seattle. They called it *Nguòi Viêt Tây Bắc,* which literally means, Vietnamese people of the Northwest."

The paper's readership grew, and so did its publication from once a week to twice a week. Julie's family's newspaper became part of her life until she pursued higher education.

In late 2008, Julie would once again return to Seattle and come back to the newspaper, this time as a co-owner. "I decided to return and learn about business first-hand by working at the newspaper. You learn a lot about business by working a small community newspaper. My younger brother, Andy, had been at the newspaper since 2003. We worked together, and we realized we wanted to drive a more aggressive business model. The only way we could do so was to buy out our parents. So, we bought the weekday edition from them. We secured a microloan from Rainier Valley Community Development Fund. I learned a lot about business just by having to write that proposal!"

So, Julie did what felt right by following her passion to be an entrepreneur while also having the peace of mind of helping her family and continuing their work for the Vietnamese community. As a result, she feels good about her choice, which contributes to her mental happiness. Oh yes, and it helps that Julie also makes time to work out. "Exercise is like therapy for me, and I make sure I work out at least once a week, if not three to four times a week. We are only given one body and we have to take care of it."

Not only are we given just one body, but we're also given just one life. Don't you think you owe it to yourself to strive to live a healthy life every day?

CHAPTER NINE

Ethnic Is Chic

You must live underneath a rock if you have never heard of Linsanity. At the time of this writing, Jeremy Lin is a professional NBA player for the New York Knicks. His is a Linderalla story. When he graduated from high school, he didn't receive an athletic scholarship to college and ended up going to Harvard to play basketball. Afterward Lin was undrafted right out of college, but later signed with the Golden State Warriors, but played very little in the 2010 season.

In the 2011 preseason, two teams, the Golden State Warriors and the Houston Rockets, waived Lin before he joined the New York Knicks. And, even then, he was on the verge of getting cut when Baron Davis was signed. Media stories say Lin was sleeping on a player's couch during this transitional period in New York City.

And, then, he got playing time. Everyone saw his raw talent and his team orientation.

Fans, the media, and the world have been fascinated by how this six-foot, three-inch Asian American basketball player can play ball, the first American player in the NBA league of Chinese or Taiwanese descent. What is amazing is that he was never given the chance to show his talents.

Born to parents who immigrated to this country from Taiwan, Lin's story of pure determination and his underdog spirit has touched many hearts, including mine. Yet his ethnicity is the conversation that is making headlines; they are about the talents of Asian Americans on the basketball court. Lin is defying stereotypes about how Asians aren't quick-footed and athletic enough to play basketball at a professional level.

Beyond sports, pho, dim sum, bubble tea, and so on are ethnic foods, cuisine, and drinks that are now mainstream. People of all ethnic backgrounds have embraced culturally rich foods, some of which have even gone American, like Korean barbecue.

I can remember a time when I was actually embarrassed to bring my Filipino food to school. I was concerned about the aroma and its presentation, which would make my Caucasian friends wince. But, over the years, ethnic foods have become much more acceptable thanks to the Internet and the media making the world smaller. (I am proud of my heritage, including Filipino food.)

With more immigrants coming to this country, there's greater access to these types of culturally diverse foods. If you tune into the Food Network, you'll find shows where the chefs show how to prepare exotic dishes from all over the world. What I thought was once peculiar is now becoming more familiar to the Western or American palate.

It's not just food that's being embraced by the general public. We are starting to see more ethnicity in the media . . . *finally*. My favorite show on primetime is *Modern Family*. One of the stars on the show is Sofia Vergara, and her TV character, Gloria, often talks about her Columbian culture, which she is proud to share—from her country's superstitions to how they celebrate holidays. She speaks with a thick accent, and sometimes she doesn't speak perfect English. And, I love it! I'm impressed that the show is allowing Gloria to embrace her heritage. Finally a show in the twenty-first century is telling the American public it's okay to be ethnic.

On the other hand, Margaret Cho's sitcom, *All-American Girl,* created in 1994, didn't have that authentic cultural feel. The show centered on her character, Margaret Kim. She was a twenty-something, modern American young woman who lived with her more traditional Korean family.

When I interviewed Margaret for *Stiletto Woman* magazine, she shared with me that the show's executives actually gave her mixed messages. At one point she was told she was "too Asian," and at other times she was coached on "not being Asian enough."

Margaret said, "It was very hard to please them. I also didn't realize how ridiculous it was [at the time]. I just wanted to keep the job. They were also complaining about my weight, about me being too fat to do the part, which was weird because I was playing myself, or the character I had created in my standup comedy routine. It didn't make any sense."

With all that confusion, the show unfortunately didn't get picked up for a second season.

Well, *Modern Family* shows that the times have changed. I'm finding that interest in culture and ethnicity is becoming more mainstream and more saleable than ever.

Understand Cultural Nuances

A partner at Deloitte, Anna Mok, said that she thinks immigrants may be much more attuned to cultural nuances. "I have become a student of them and have a deep understanding of these kinds of things, whether it's something unspoken or an appreciation for how people interact and their dynamics with one another."

What she sees as the major cultural nuance is that many Pan Asian immigrants tend to have a deep regard for social hierarchy when it comes to how they view and interact with their bosses. "We have a respect for our elders and demonstrate that respect in very different ways than the typical non-Asian," Anna said. "In many Asian homes, filial piety, the notion of complete and total respect for our family, especially our elders, runs very deep. How you respect your elders, by not questioning parental decisions and by not arguing with your parents in public, is one of a host of traits in the Pan Asian culture that often extends into the workplace."

In addition, Anna likes to use her tea and water example. When Anna goes to dinner with Asians, especially Chinese, it's customary to fill other people's cups starting with the oldest at the table, with hers being the last to fill. "Pouring tea for the elders at the table is a way to show your respect."

But, she doesn't do it all the time. She said it depends on her audience. "My cultural tendency is to show respect for everyone in the room. But it's a trait I have to be mindful of and one I could still choose to demonstrate, but someone could have a different opinion of me because they may not view my actions as signs of respect but instead interpret them as being subservient. You have to assess the room or situation and understand the context of how your actions will be interpreted."

And, as an Asian American female executive, Anna is also often asked, "Where are you from?" She frequently says San Francisco, where she grew up. But, when the person asking has an unsatisfied look, she understands that they really want to know her ethnic background. She doesn't find that question offensive because she wasn't born in the US, but can understand why an American-born Asian may react differently. Anna thinks, in general, people often ask out of curiosity and a desire to find common ground and not out of ignorance or disrespect.

Know Your Audience

And, if you need help understanding cultural differences, it's time that you brush up on your societal 101 skills. That's what I did, by attending an event hosted by Ascend for Nancy Mueller, CEO of International Adaptation. She helps global executives polish their personal brand through communication and social skills. Her clients are among the top performers in their respective fields and include The Boeing Company, Coca-Cola Enterprises, Weyerhaeuser, and many more.

Nancy is also the author of *Work Worldwide: International Career Strategies for the Adventurous Job Seeker* (Avalon Travel Publications), a book that's described as a "nuts-and-bolts excellent" guide for finding your dream assignment abroad.

As someone who is an avid world traveler, writer, and teacher, Nancy has seen her fair share of different cultural perspectives, like when it comes to time and punctuality.

Time

"In general, business professionals around the globe are expected to be on time for appointments. But some cultures are more relaxed about being a few minutes late than others," Nancy said.

"For example, in the US, if your interview is scheduled for 2:00 P.M., you are expected to arrive by that time. If you show up late, it gives a negative impression, and the interviewer may wonder if she or he can depend on you in other situations. But if you were to arrive a few minutes late for an appointment in Brazil or Egypt, there is more latitude, and it doesn't typically create a negative impression as it does in the US or China, for instance."

Formality

She also has seen that formality is another cultural nuance that comes into play. "Americans value informality and like to get on a first-name basis with people they've just met as quickly as possible. Less attention is paid to rank and status. As an example, an American friend of mine described meeting a South Korean businessman for the first time. He introduced himself to the Korean and said, "You can call me Peter. What should I call you?" The Korean businessman answered, "Professor Kim."

This advice also applies to Americans visiting other countries. A writer friend of mine was hosted in China by some very influential business associates, and, because he is a friendly kind of guy, he treated everyone on an equal basis. Finally, he was told by his hosts to be more reserved and less "friendly."

As for Russian business etiquette, Nancy said, "Russians tend to be more formal in their dress and relationships than are Americans. Like Asians, Russians respect age, rank, and title. Hierarchy matters. However, they are more expressive and confrontational in their communications than are Asians, generally speaking."

Communication

In India, she was brought in as a consultant by a firm due to a breakdown in communication between a US Caucasian manager and an East Indian employee. The conflict was a misunderstanding around the expectations of roles and positions of authority. "The employee had deferred to his boss in a crisis situation when his boss had expected him to use his own initiative to solve the problem. It wasn't that the employee couldn't solve the problem, but that's what he would have done in India, because the bosses' ranks and titles are respected."

According to Nancy, it's important to understand cultural differences in corporate and business settings, or it could lead to disastrous business errors. "Culture affects workplace attitudes and behaviors in a variety of ways: decision making, the role of boss and subordinate, hiring new employees or selecting new business partners, resolving conflicts, negotiations and meeting styles, work hours, socializing, speaking up at meetings, and work/life benefits. Without cultural awareness, professionals run the risk of making assumptions and decisions about others based on their own cultural filters, which can result in costly business blunders."

If you aren't a world traveler, have never worked in a different culture, or have never been exposed to people of diverse backgrounds, Nancy recommends doing your homework to build successful cross-cultural relationships. "One good resource is the *Dun & Bradstreet's Guide to Doing Business Around the World.* I also recommend talking with associates who have had experience dealing with clients and customers from different cultures, as well as individuals who come from multicultural backgrounds and families."

With companies looking overseas to do business, especially in Asia, Vanna Novak, the president and owner of Speak to Persuade, said being someone from a particular country or that part of the world makes you more marketable because you understand the culture and can possibly speak the language. Despite this positive traction and upward mobility, with ethnic people now viewed as emerging leaders, there are unfortunately still stereotypes out there.

Recognize Where the Stereotypes Started

Vanna believes the stereotypes come from several sources. "One is from the people who are around us while growing up—whether that is parents or family members or their friends, or even classmates and teachers. In particular, anybody who served as an authority figure in our lives while growing up." Vanna goes on to say that our direct experience with different groups of people of color can also shape our opinion. "I think oftentimes what happens is our experiences are colored—no pun intended—and we buy into our family's beliefs during our early formidable years. It happens a lot through early messages from those around us as we are becoming the person we are meant to be."

And she also said the media have a strong influence shaping and forming our opinions.

When I listened to James Sun, a Korean immigrant, who spoke at the 2011 Seattle Annual Ascend Gala, he shared with the audience that when he became a finalist out of 800,000 people who auditioned for season six of *The Apprentice*, he had to convince the producers that Asians do make good TV . . . if given the opportunity.

Producers flew him and the other finalists to Los Angeles where they were sequestered for a week and went through an intense interview process. James met with producers. They asked him, "Why should we have you on the show?"

He remembers thinking about this question very carefully and posed the question back to the producers. "I know there are a lot of Asians who are good business people, but in the six seasons that you've done *The Apprentice*, you've never had one Asian male contestant on the show. Why is that?"

James remembers the room getting quiet, and finally one of the producers said, "James, you want the honest truth?"

James said, "Of course I do."

"Asians really don't make good TV, especially Asian men," said the producer.

James remembers being floored by that comment. It made him mad, and he didn't know if the producers were just trying to get a reaction from him. To actually hear that from the producers, James saw first-hand how TV really worked, and this exposed the stereotypes around casting Asians, especially when producers added, "Most Asians are quiet and good at math," which in their mind doesn't make for good primetime ratings.

This man, who was the CEO of a company, somehow convinced the producers to give him a shot. So, when he got on the show, James intentionally chose not to do any stereotypical tasks associated with

Asians, like accounting or math projects, or being the computer guy. He intentionally chose to take on creative roles like marketing. "I took a more vocal leadership role than being a background leader." His plan worked because James became the runner-up for the show that year. Most importantly, James showed millions of Americans that Asians do make great TV.

Be You

And someone who also has seen stereotypes is Bruno Singh.

As the NBCUniversal vice president, Bruno said it took him a while to find the balance between American culture and the values of his home country, India, a challenge his family has faced for the last forty years. "In becoming an effective leader, I've tried to evolve my American-centric extroversion skills while maintaining the calm and peace my culture and religion teach me. This is not easy, and I get challenged everyday with the potential conflict." He said it doesn't help that there is a lack of role models for a young person seeking guidance in corporate America right now.

As a Sikhism follower (Sikhism is a religion formed in Northwest India about 500 years ago), Bruno adheres to a monotheistic belief system when it comes to serving others. The religion espouses spirituality and meditation. The founders of Sikhism have assigned some daily rituals, like not cutting one's hair and wearing a turban, to identify its followers. Bruno said not every Sikh follows the religion as closely as he does. "It's a link to a vibrant and proud heritage that reminds me every day to improve myself in some small way."

One small way for Bruno is wearing a turban. When I saw him receive an "Ascend Inspirational Leader" award at the national conference in 2011, he proudly wore a red turban with his suit.

This immigrant from Punjab in Northwest India, known for farming, entrepreneurship, and dancing, has remained true to Sikhism even though his family migrated to this country when he was just eight years old.

His father was an electrical engineer. Growing up with a family who embraced technology, Bruno saw that computer science was a field that's robust with lots of career opportunities. It was a natural fit for him to go into the information technology field. In 1999, he came to NBCUniversal as a senior director of IT services. Four years later, he was promoted to vice president.

As an Asian man in an executive position, Bruno wears a turban. He doesn't find people forming stereotypes about him because of his headwear. Instead, the stereotypes revolve around Asian personality traits such as being detail-oriented, dependable, stable, trustworthy, honorable, and compliant. Bruno believes those are good qualities to have, but not if you are seeking a leadership position. "Unfortunately, these are not the traits that leaders require in the US. Desirable traits include extroversion, risk-taking, and being communicative and demonstrative when needed."

He said in order to overcome these cultural biases, you begin by changing yourself. "The stereotyping will only dissipate once Asian leaders exhibit the desired traits in vast numbers. We are short of role models in this arena."

To overcome these stereotypes, Bruno said you begin by being your authentic self in your communication and presentation skills. For example, the general stereotype of Pan Asians is of being conservative and lackluster. When I had dinner with Bruno, I found that he is one Asian that doesn't fit that mold. And, he said this had to do with being selected to participate in a GE leadership program in 2006, which helped him become a more effective leader. The class taught him to uncover his own personal style in a leadership role. He didn't want to be seen as someone who strictly goes by the books, but who has the ability to formulate his own thoughts and opinions from his authentic voice. From interacting with Bruno, I can say that he is a witty and funny guy. Bruno learned that it's okay to have that communication style. It has made him connect better with customers, peers, and staff. "People around me now feel they 'know' my true self."

As an Asian male, Bruno learned how to overcome the stereotypes that came with his gender and background. But imagine, if you are the doctor of the US president, do you get a hall pass for any preconceived ideas? Not if you are an attractive, petite immigrant woman.

Titles Sometimes Are Overlooked

As I shared earlier, Dr. Connie Mariano, former head of the White House Medical Unit, faced stereotypes on the job. As a doctor to three presidents, Dr. Mariano was constantly underestimated because of her looks. "People would assume I didn't speak English. When I told them I was in the navy, they assumed I was enlisted and not an officer. When I told them I was in the health care profession, they assumed I was a nurse and not a doctor." She often finds herself educating people that their stereotypes and assumptions are wrong. In this regard, she said, actions speak louder than words, so Dr. Mariano makes sure she is giving her best all the time and in every situation.

This means focusing on being a good leader and taking care of the troops and accomplishing the mission at hand. She has this advice for those who may find themselves in similar situations. "Ignore the stereotypes. Find and listen to your own voice. Believe in yourself. Don't take no for an answer. Women who feel uncomfortable entering a room and finding they 'stand out' from the crowd, take comfort in knowing that this is your chance to be OUT-standing!"

I believe her book, *The White House Doctor*, which tells the inspirational tale of this daughter of a Filipino Navy steward, who as a child helped her father prepare dinner on Christmas for admirals and who became a rear admiral herself, is a must read for all immigrants, especially Pan Asian women. As quoted above, she tells numerous stories of having to fight against stereotypes throughout her career as an Asian woman, a doctor, and even as a female naval officer. It is also very witty and funny, another "nontypical" Asian trait.

Learn to Adapt to American Culture

One who knows how to be outstanding is my boss at RealSelf, Maureen Ezekwugo, who is half-Korean and half-Caucasian. Maureen E.'s mom has always instilled in her the importance of respecting people who are older than her who have authority, and this includes the men in her life. This meant that Maureen E. shouldn't address them by their first name. Older people were categorized as either "older sister" or "older brother." A sign of respect meant bowing when saying hello or thank you.

"When I was young, I even saw my mom refrain from drinking an occasional glass of wine in front of her brothers and father because it was disrespectful for women to drink in front of older men," said Maureen E. She adds, "The Korean culture also insists on modesty—so I didn't grow up in an environment where people were showing off or boasting about their accomplishments. I saw consistent hard work being rewarded and admired as qualities that I should emulate and follow."

But as Maureen E. reflects on her career, there are things she would have done differently. She realized that the traditions of her Asian heritage influenced her communication and negotiation styles when it came to work challenges and solutions. While it didn't prevent her from producing great results throughout her career, she's conscious that her traditional reticence held her back. "There were many times where I didn't push ideas that I strongly believed in hard enough because somewhere inside of my Asian-self I believed, 'If someone with authority is telling me it should be another way, I need to respect that.'"

Maureen E. also recognized that, unlike her Caucasian American counterparts, she wasn't one to brag about her accomplishments or accept praise from others. "I often downplayed my accomplishments, giving credit to others or attributing my success to something else. I felt my hard work and results would speak for themselves."

"Meanwhile, I watched many others, who didn't work as hard as me and who produced less results, move ahead of me because they were more vocal about what they did, regardless of how small the accomplishment. I also saw other leaders around me sometimes get credit for some of my ideas because I chose to defer to authority and let them push the ideas through."

What's ironic is that Maureen E. expects the complete opposite from the people who report to her. She wants them to speak up and respects that. "I like it when I'm challenged by someone on my team who gets me to see something in a different way. I like it when my team members are proud of their accomplishments and can celebrate their wins. Yet I don't always apply the same rules to myself."

Maureen E. is conscious of this tendency and is constantly pushing herself out of her comfort zone so these cultural beliefs don't hold her back.

(I work for Maureen E., and I can tell you that I'm not shy about self-promotion as long as it's done in an appropriate manner and isn't obnoxious.)

As someone who has hired hundreds of people, she has also seen how the humble approach from someone with a traditional Asian upbringing can work against potential job candidates in an interview. They are reserved and find it difficult to describe their accomplishments and speak in an authentic way about who they are and what assets they can bring to the company. "My advice to these people is to embrace the obstacles they've overcome, which have made them who they are, and learn to freely talk about how they faced a challenge and overcame it. Perseverance and determination can set you apart very distinctly from another candidate with the same skill set."

Hispanic and Latino Stereotyping

Another person from an immigrant family who has also set himself apart is Richard Velazquez. I met him through various networking events in Seattle. At the time of this interview, he has just accepted a position as "senior director of strategic innovations—technology" for PepsiCo in New York. He's focused on driving innovation in the vending machine industry to make the equipment and experience more engaging and fun for consumers while being profitable for businesses. If anybody can, it's Richard. He's a guy who has come a long way.

Richard's parents moved to Brooklyn, New York, from Puerto Rico for more opportunities. He came from humble beginnings, growing up in a public housing apartment complex that was frequently infested with cockroaches and mice. Born in the ghetto, he never let life's challenges get in his way, even when his parents couldn't afford to help pay for his college. Richard found a way.

He is an excellent role model for anybody, in particular Latinos and Hispanics. You may wonder, what is the difference between Latinos and Hispanics? And, what about Mexicans? Being the co-founder of the Seattle chapter of the National Society of Hispanic MBAs or NSHMBA, Richard is the guy to explain these distinctions and their cultural differences.

First, let's begin with the definition used in the 2010 Census.

"'Hispanic or Latino' refers to a person of Cuban, Mexican, Puerto Rican, South or Central American, or other Spanish culture or origin regardless of race."

To Richard, Hispanic is anyone from or with ancestry from Spanish-speaking countries (Mexico, Central and South America, Spain, and Caribbean Islands such as Puerto Rico or Cuba).

Latino is anyone with origins from Latin America or territories in the Caribbean where Spanish or Portuguese prevail (which, in this case, would include Brazilians, which are not technically Hispanic, but it would not include Spain).

According to Richard, "There is a great deal of overlap between the two terms, which is why a lot of people use them interchangeably (including the US Census). I am technically both Latino and Hispanic as both of my parents were born in Puerto Rico." (Richard was born in Brooklyn, New York.)

The 2010 US Census reports that there were roughly 50.5 million people of Latino/Hispanic origin, or just over 16 percent of the total US population.

From Richard's experience, he has found that stereotypes about Latinos and Hispanics are more prevalent in cities with lower Hispanic populations than in those with high Hispanic populations, such as New York City, Miami, or San Jose, California. In fact, Richard said, he's experienced many of these stereotypes from business professionals in large corporations throughout his tenure at both NSHMBA and the Society of Hispanic Professional Engineers (SHPE).

In Richard's words, here are the most common stereotypes he's faced:

Stereotype #1: Hispanic = Mexican

As discussed above, Hispanics can originate from a great many countries. Given Mexico's size and proximity to the US, the vast majority of US Hispanics have Mexican origins. From the 2006 American Community Survey, 64 percent of US Hispanics were Mexican. The next biggest group was Puerto Ricans with less than 10 percent of the US Hispanic population.

This leads to the stereotype that "Hispanic" is synonymous with "Mexican." I've planned dozens of events for major corporations for both SHPE and NSHMBA over the years, and many times the corporate sponsors want to develop a Hispanic-themed event to connect with the target audience. The first thing out of their mouths is "Let's do a Cinco de Mayo theme for the event!" I've had to point out to them that not all Hispanics are Mexican, and a more culturally broad event might resonate better with the whole audience.

A good example of this nuance comes from my corporate experience with Procter and Gamble in Puerto Rico, which focused on US Hispanic marketing. There are several Spanish-speaking countries whose citizens don't respond well to a Mexican accent. Thus, when we were shooting a commercial for Downy that used Mexican children, we had to dub over their voices with a more neutral Spanish-accent in demographic areas that were more heavily populated with non-Mexican Hispanics. Focus group testing showed a very negative reaction to these accents because participants felt these corporations assumed all Hispanics were Mexican and therefore did not understand their unique cultural differences.

Stereotype #2: Hispanic = Immigrant, or Pro-Illegal Immigration

Due in part to the first stereotype above and the large number of Hispanics with Mexican origin, I've also come across a lot of stereotypes surrounding Hispanics and immigration.

I've ceased to be surprised by how many people outside of New York don't realize that Puerto Rico is a US commonwealth, which means that every Puerto Rican is a US citizen and does not need to immigrate to the US. Recently, a reporter for a major publication inadvertently highlighted this lack of awareness in an article that discussed President Obama's visit to Puerto Rico as part of a news story on immigration reform. Every Puerto Rican born in Puerto Rico can get a US Passport and travel freely throughout the US without a visa. Puerto Ricans living on the island can't vote for the US president and don't pay federal taxes but otherwise have all the rights and privileges of a US citizen.

The other stereotype is that if you're Hispanic, you probably support or condone illegal immigration. As mentioned above, because of Puerto

Rico's unique status among all of the Spanish-speaking countries, the immigration debate is not as relevant to Puerto Ricans as it might be to the Mexican-American community. Even among non-Puerto Rican Hispanics (including Mexicans), not everyone believes or condones illegal immigration, probably most notably among South Americans who have gone through the legal channels to gain citizenship. So, while views about immigration vary widely among Hispanics, the common thread I have seen is the need for immigration reform.

Stereotype #3: All Hispanics Speak Spanish

There is a great deal of diversity among Hispanics in the US, and that includes language preference. I would say there are three types of Hispanics with regards to language—English dominant, Spanish dominant, and those who prefer English and Spanish equally. I consider myself English dominant, even though I'm fairly fluent in Spanish. I worked with a former executive board member of NSHMBA Seattle who was of Mexican descent but didn't speak a word of Spanish (so, it could be English dominant or English only). Realizing these differences among US Hispanics, Albert Torres, the CEO and publisher of the Hispanic-targeted *tú Decides* in Washington, launched his newspaper with one side in English and the other in Spanish (tú Decides stands for "You Decide").

Hopefully, taking Richard's suggestion when you go to a restaurant that serves Hispanic or Latino food, you can also appreciate the culture more.

With this diversity perspective, you'll have a deeper understanding of people's backgrounds and be respectful of their customs. Furthermore, you will make an even more memorable impression if you actually assimilate some cultural nuances. Perhaps, you'll be more open to pouring other people's drinks if you are surrounded by traditional Asians. And, if you are someone with years of leadership experience, you can act as a mentor to an upcoming star. As Bruno said, there's a need for mentors in the Pan Asian communities.

If you're someone with a diverse background, is there a piece of your heritage that's holding you back from getting a job or a promotion? How will you be able to blend your ethnicity with the Western ways? It's all about you being self-aware and negotiating with yourself on what to bring into the office, and what's best to maybe leave in a personal setting.

CHAPTER TEN

Live a Balanced Life

I've shared with you throughout this entire journey the importance of working hard, putting your nose to the grindstone, and making some sacrifices in order to achieve your goals. But I also want you to remember the importance of living a balanced life. Why? It's the best way to keep your energy level at a pitch. My CEO at RealSelf works ten to twelve hours a day, but he always makes time for his yoga class so he can "Zen" out when he deals with his employees. Another friend, who's a salesman and drives all day, volunteers as an assistant wrestling coach at night so he doesn't burn out. And on weekends, both men also recharge their batteries by going out in nature, and not by sitting in front of the "boob tube."

I know a rap artist who works seven days a week, but he schedules getaway weekends with his wife to keep balanced while pursuing his passion in the cutthroat music industry. Spending time with loved ones and tending to their needs, even if you have to hire a nanny, connect us to the greater whole. Self-interest is not the key to success; it's doing it for others, especially family. It's a lesson many of us learn too late in life.

But it's not just balancing work with personal interests, but with all aspects of life. Take parenting for example.

Tiger Mother

I had a chance to interview Amy Chua, the author of the controversial memoir, *The Battle Hymn of the Tiger Mother*. This was one year after her book came out. Ironically, the interview happened on Friday, January 13. It was actually a day that brought Amy good luck as she came to Bothell, Washington to sign copies of the book's paperback edition. But she admitted, "It's been a tough year."

The water cooler talk about Amy's memoir pushed it onto *The New York Times* bestseller's list. More than 100 people came to listen to the infamous mom's firestorm year, after a newspaper excerpt mischaracterized her book. "I was asked to defend a book I didn't write. It was difficult to do interviews."

Last January, the *Wall Street Journal* published an excerpt titled "Why Chinese Mothers Are Superior." It talked about what Amy would never allow her daughters Sophia and Louisa (nicknamed "Lulu") to do. Here are a few examples:

- attend a sleepover
- have a play date
- be in a school play
- choose their own extracurricular activities

Amy still can't shake the *WSJ* headline that generated 500,000 Internet hits within hours and painted her as a bad mother. "That was the most painful thing," said Amy, who felt misunderstood by people who just read the excerpt and never read the book.

She reminded the audience the book was never designed to be a how-to parenting guide, but a memoir making fun of her and the strict parenting approach of her immigrant parents.

Amy went on to tell the crowd that the tongue-and-cheek book is being marketed differently in China, where the title was translated to *Parenting by a Yale Professor: How to Raise Kids in America*. Wearing five-inch stiletto shoes, black skirt, tights, and a flower blouse, she said moms in China even come up to her for make-up tips for their daughters.

The audience laughed.

The controversy wasn't a laughing matter for her, though. Amy is a professor of law at Yale Law School. When the backlash surrounding her memoir erupted, Amy thought, "Oh God, I have to quit my job. What happens if they [students] boycott my class and nobody comes?" But, the opposite happened. Her students threw her a party, and she earned an award for Best Teacher, which Amy said is very difficult to get at Yale.

Don't expect the three-time published author to write a sequel of her memoir anytime soon. Her next project is an academic book.

Would this Tiger Mother do anything over? "Sometimes I wonder if I should not have included some of those lines that got me in so much trouble. But then it would not have been an honest book." She goes on to say, "What really matters is what my girls think of me."

According to Amy, the memoir has brought them closer. Her older daughter, Sophia, wrote an article for the *New York Post* defending her mother. She is now a student at Harvard. As for Lulu, she plays tennis in high school, an extracurricular activity that Amy didn't warm up to at first. (Remember Amy's rules?)

The overbearing mom loosened up when Lulu rebelled. This forced Amy to take a hard look at balancing Asian and Western childrearing methods. Amy said, "*Battle Hymn* is about me almost losing my daughter [Lulu]."

Amy pulled back from her strict parenting and made compromises with Lulu, who was thirteen years old at that time.

The softer mom said, "I do think traditional Asian culture, and I use that term very loosely, is hard work and requires self-discipline . . . the bad part is that it's too narrow and too stifling and too oppressive." She went on to say that the Western parenting style, another term she uses loosely, allows for creativity and independence.

"If you were to ask me what the best approach is, I would say it is balance," Amy said. This is combining the work ethic and self-discipline with rebellion and thinking outside of the box, and constantly pushing and pulling between the two.

Whether you're a fan of *Tiger Mother* or not, the book created an international discussion regarding parenting styles. "Parenthood is too complex to simplify down to what is right for every child and situation," said John Tran, a Seattle counselor. "If there was a right way, we'd all be well-adjusted adults!"

You might also find yourself in Amy's situation, in that constant tug-of-war as a parent of how to blend "Eastern" and "Western" cultures. How do you raise your children so they keep their birth country's values in their new homeland? As Amy shared, it takes some growing pains.

Another immigrant famly had other issues: how to move the entire family to their new homeland. They soon realized it would not be an easy move.

Balance Sections of Your Life

Emily Rollins is an assurance partner at Deloitte, a journey that took her fourteen years after graduating from college to complete. She could have moved faster on her climb in corporate America, but she wanted to start a family at the same time. She learned from her father, "[That] with passion, dedication, and good health, as long as you prioritize what's most valuable to you, there will be a time for everything else."

When she was just a year old, Emily's dad and mom came to America in search of better opportunities, leaving her sister and her in the Philippines with their grandparents so her parents could establish themselves in the United States. A US executive sponsored her dad. And, he knew at that time that he had to make this sacrifice in order to improve the lives of his family in the future. He knew he would soon "balance" work and family and make it up to his daughters.

His game plan worked. A year later, he brought the rest of the family over to the States. Emily learned that you cannot always do everything according to your game plan, but oftentimes you have to make sacrifices along the way, and balancing priorities like her father did is the key.

In college, Emily focused on grooming her skills and expanding her mind. When she graduated from Claremont McKenna College, she then wanted to start a family, and, at the same time, also establish her career. This was a time Emily could've charged hard—work now, family later. However, she realized that with her mother's help watching her children, she could do both. But she wanted to work part-time, which was not common in her profession back then. That would also mean that other people might surpass her with promotions, but Emily was okay with this decision. It was hers, and she understood that was what would make her happy and whole. Eventually, Deloitte admitted her to the partnership about two years behind her peers. Emily has no regrets. "What's really important to keep in mind is that life comes in stages."

As her four children got older, Emily and her husband made the decision that she would work full-time, and he would stay at home to homeschool their children. This made sense for them at that time. "I learned to let some things go that weren't really important, like a spotless kitchen and taking dance classes. However, what was important was that I had a husband who valued the same things as I did and that I worked for a firm that valued me and my potential and was flexible during the different phases of my life."

Unfortunately for Dr. Connie Mariano, the pressure of being a physician to the president was a real strain for her and her family. "I came home late at night or in the early hours of the morning and would leave early in the day. Most of the time when I saw my children, they were asleep. My husband and I shared very little during the time I worked for the president. He stayed home and cared for the kids. It ultimately killed my marriage, and we divorced seven years later."

When Dr. Mariano retired from the navy after her years as the White House doctor, she and her family moved to Scottsdale, Arizona, where she did get to spend more time with her children and husband. She took a position at the Mayo Clinic that wasn't so time consuming and allowed her be with her two boys, but by then, her marriage was on the rocks.

Balancing career and family isn't easy. Neither Emily's nor Dr. Mariano's game plan to do both were foolproof, and in Dr. Mariano's case did not lead to a happier and successful marriage. What I've learned from these successful immigrant women is that it's hard to have a balanced life regardless of how much planning and thought are put into the mix. You can only do your best. And, what I do appreciate is that both women had careers in addition to having a family. They learned the hard lessons about "balancing" their home and work life and what can happen when you don't.

For me, it's been tough to balance having a significant other and juggling my many projects. I do feel like I am married to my work. But, then I realize, if I were to marry and have a family, I wouldn't have the time to do so much. At this stage in my life, I have the freedom to charge hard in my career. As I write this final chapter of my book, I am single, and I have amazing friends. With Emily's advice, I'm taking life in stages.

This is not to say that I can't have it all. I can. I just will need help or a flexible guy who will work with me to juggle everything.

For now, not being married and not having kids, I don't have to face tough decisions like Emily and Dr. Mariano. And with Emily's advice, the time will come when I "settle down" to have my family. I'm taking life in stages.

Right now, this stage in my life is career. Apparently, I'm not alone.

Seize the Opportunity

For Englishman Stewart, when an opportunity arose to move across the pond, he didn't hesitate, even though the decision came with a lot of stress. For one, he is taking a performance-based job. "If I lose my job, I lose my visa and thus, I move on. By moving on, I lose the commitment and sacrifices I have made to move here in the first place." Yet the rewards outweighed the risk for Stewart.

Single, no kids, and thirty-four years old, he had the freedom to take the job opening as a vice president relationship manager for a bank in Seattle. Working abroad isn't something new for this rising star. Stewart has lived in three previous countries, all in Asia. He's always had the itch to live and work in America, and knew accepting this position would only add to his résumé and develop his business acumen. "In my role in international finance and banking, I see that the world is changing and that US businesses will need to adapt, particularly internationally. How they successfully interact abroad will determine any significant growth for them." He knows moving to this country and witnessing firsthand how American business emerges as a leader in a slumping world economy makes this the best place to be.

Stewart also gets to be exposed to the American culture, something he's had a fascination with. "Positive, innovative, and 'can do' are cultural traits of the US that are not universal, and thus being immersed in them will improve me."

Despite the United States facing a high unemployment rate at the time, Stewart made his move to this country at the end of 2011, because the US is still the largest economy in the world. "The US has remarkable entrepreneurs and businesses. To see this firsthand is both fascinating and beneficial. My interest and experience is in the specialty field of international business, and particularly China. China and the US are key countries as we move through the twenty-first century. I have seen China but not the US, and it makes sense to understand both."

While the move to America is certainly making Stewart much more marketable professionally and will improve his global business résumé, he can't help but second-guess his decision at times. He has parents who are getting older, and he worries about them. "I wonder if I am selfish, and whether or not I will regret the missed time with them."

Stewart's memories of his parents are fond ones, despite that he hardly saw his father growing up as he worked to provide for the family. Eventually, his father started his own company with his grandfather to manufacture knives and tooling equipment for the cobbler industry and beyond. His mum worked as a food hygienist before becoming the company secretary with the family firm. Yet, he remembers a childhood where it was a safe and fun environment, and with the UK providing a great education and healthcare system. Again, for now, he is taking life in stages with career in the forefront. (When his aging parents need his help more, that's a decision he'll make then.)

If you do get a position to make that move later on in life to a new homeland, Stewart had this advice:

- You need to work hard to find the opportunity (unless you are lucky) and/or accept that it will not be perfect and thus be prepared for the changes.
- Do you have the right character for a new place? Evaluate what type of person succeeds and if you fit that profile. Different places may require different characters.
- I have always had the view that, although I may have an opinion, as a guest of a country I need to respect the culture and history that has developed the status quo. It is therefore neither right nor wrong, just different.

Stewart understands that any change, whether moving to a new country, accepting a new job, or beginning a new phase in life, can be stressful, and offers this thought: "Departmentalize issues, deal with them, don't worry for worry's sake, and move on. Oh, and really enjoy life as much as you can. Smile and the world will smile back."

What Does Balance Mean to You?

As you see from Stewart's story, balance means something different for everyone. For Stewart, balance as being culturally aware and sharp in business. For Emily, balance is about the different "stages in life." And now, let's take a look at balance when it comes to work. Thach Nguyen, a self-made millionaire through real estate ventures, remembers his immigrant parents working hard to provide for him and his four brothers and sister. With just the clothes on their back and twenty dollars, Thach's dad brought his family to America. He felt a lot of pressure to succeed, like with most immigrant families. This is the reason for the hard work and hunger to do well in this country—failure isn't an option with so many people depending on you. That is why Thach appreciates the work ethic of many immigrant families. But, he said, he sees too often that immigrant workers don't take the time to really enjoy life or spend time with their families. Thach said, "I want to be successful, don't get me wrong. But they sacrifice their soul, their family, their blood for success, which to me is not real success."

His definition of success hit Thach when his father passed away. With the wealth he acquired, the real estate agent decided to give back to his community, whether through financial contributions, providing affordable housing for those in need, or speaking for various organizations about leading a balanced life. While he is successful at what he does, to Thach, life isn't all about making money. To him, a balanced life means "the level of our happiness is in direct proportion to the number of people we are serving." That means if Thach hasn't set aside a certain amount of his earnings for his philanthropic work, then he doesn't feel successful.

Distribution of Assets

Since we are on the topic of money, let me recall an earlier chapter where I shared how Grandma Mary survived the Great Depression but passed away due to a stroke. I knew she was a savvy businesswoman, but I didn't know how astute. You see, when Grandma was alive and we had lunch, she'd never spent more than $11.00 on a meal. She always insisted on paying for her own meal when we went out as a family. I never saw or heard Grandma say, "Let me treat the family." She was very conservative with her cash.

So, when my grandmother passed on, I had no idea that she had four houses fully paid off and some cash to give to her immediate family. It blew me away. Yet, I felt a bit guilty taking it because I would've liked to have used that money for more experiences with my grandma while she was alive. It made me think, did my grandma ever spoil herself? I never saw her take lavish trips or buy an expensive car. When she did make a car purchase, it was always a second-hand vehicle. Of course, I saw Grandma get her nails and hair done, but she certainly didn't live the life I have when she was my age.

For my grandmother's last birthday, she wouldn't let us throw her a big party and spend any money on her. She insisted: no birthday party. I think she felt guilty letting us treat her, but I wish she hadn't. It brought us joy to spend money on her. I sometimes wish Grandma did allow herself to have a little bit more fun.

She was always very responsible and never lived beyond her means. And, I am certainly still learning that lesson from my grandma even if she isn't here. Before I make a purchase, I think: *Do I really need it? Will I have the financial freedom during my senior years to never be a burden on my family?* I think that's the important lesson I learned from my grandma—to be an independent woman no matter what age or stage in life. That's the "balance" I negotiate with myself when it comes to money. *It's okay to spoil myself, but am I being responsible like Grandma Mary?*

I do believe she was happy, because like Thach, Grandma Mary didn't need material things. She was happy to be a grandmother and a great-grandmother too. Again, this book would not have been possible financially without the help of my grandmother. For that, I thank her for helping make one of the biggest dreams of my life come true.

So, if you are an immigrant or you came from humble beginnings, it's likely you live Grandma Mary's lifestyle—save more than you spend. This is something you might hear from Dave Ramsey (daveramsey.com), a financial talk-show host who gives great advice on financial peace. Just keep in mind though that it is okay to let yourself have some fun and not feel guilty about it if you have the financial means to do so.

Allow Yourself Some Fun

My mom has worked so hard helping me get off on the right foot in life and also funding many of my cousins' further education. It's nice that in her fifties, I am seeing her have some fun now. I think she's actually having more fun than I am (just watch us paint the town on Friday night).

At this point in her life, my mom has a very active social calendar with friends and family. Before, she worked hard so she could save money to further my life as well as the lives of her extended family. Holidays in my childhood often saw Mom absent because she was working. Now, in my adult life, such holidays have become memorable.

She is seeing the fruits of her labor now that her children are self-sufficient. This is giving my mom permission to have fun in her life where she can travel, spoil her grandchildren, and even go out with me as a friend. Maybe, if you have obligations, it is impossible to have a "balanced" life all at once unless you have the financial means to make it happen. But I see the importance at least of striving to have one.

Another person I know who is striving to have a more balanced life is the mom of a professional fighter.

She's a "Smooth" Mom

The saying goes: Like father, like son. How about: Like son, like mother?

At four foot eleven and at fifty-one years of age, Song Henderson had just signed up for Brazilian Jiu-Jitsu, (BJJ) a martial arts with a focus on grappling and ground fighting. This is something she never imagined she would do. But with some arm-twisting [no pun intended], she's giving BJJ a shot.

Song said the instructors know her son, "So they said, 'We'll do half the price.'"

Her son is Benson Henderson, known to many as Ben "Smooth" Henderson, the new UFC lightweight champion. Ben took the title from Frankie Edgar on February 26, 2012 in a five-round main event in Saitama, Japan. Song was there watching her son fight. "I didn't get nervous," she says.

It took the Federal Way mom some time to get used to her son being a professional fighter. Ben now lives and trains in Arizona.

With a wrestling scholarship at Dana College in Nebraska and a double major in criminal justice and sociology, Ben was on his way to becoming a police officer. But Ben told his mom he wanted to be a fighter instead. "I told him, 'I don't like it. I want you to have a normal life . . . not hitting people,'" said Song.

It didn't help when Ben told his mom that his first fight only earned him $150.

"That's $150?" Song laughed. She remembers telling her son that if he became a police officer, he would earn $3,000 to $4,000 a month and it would be a "regular job." But Ben told his mom that he was still young and that he enjoyed the sport. He said he could always become a police officer after retiring from fighting.

Ironically, it's Song who initially introduced Ben to the world of martial arts. When Ben was in the fourth grade, his Korean-born mother signed him up along with his older brother, Julius, for Tae Kwon Do. Song wanted her sons to know self-defense. "I can't follow them everywhere, especially since they are boys."

Song remembers her sons earning a black belt in Tae Kwon Do two to three years after taking classes. So, when the family moved from Lynnwood to Federal Way, she was disappointed when instructors there told her that her sons had to start all over again. Song couldn't afford the classes.

Fortunately for Ben, a coach at Decatur High School recruited him to join the wrestling team. The rest is history.

You'll find pictures of Ben during his wrestling days at Song's store, Peter's Grocery on South 38th Street in Tacoma. The walls are covered with posters of her son's fights over the years.

Outside the store, a hanging banner reads: "CONGRATULATIONS! Ben "Smooth" Henderson *WEC Lightweight Champion of the World," a title he earned back in 2011 when he beat Donald "Cowboy" Cerrone.

Occasionally, Song said, you may even find Ben working behind the counter to give her a break. Song works almost seven days a week.

But she said it's different than when her sons were growing up. She was often pulling eighteen-hour workdays, juggling two jobs by working at a fast-food restaurant and dry-cleaning business. "Sometimes I feel sorry for them. I am not there for them." But Song knew it was the only way to provide for them because their father was an inconsistent presence in their lives.

Those memories bring tears to Song's eyes. She says she doesn't want her boys to deal with the same struggles she has faced. She tells her boys, "You guys marry. I don't want your wife to work. I want them to stay with the kids."

Song isn't eager for grandchildren anytime soon. She is excited though for the rematch fight between her son and Frankie. In the title fight, Song said, Ben was close to knocking Frankie out, but time ran out. In the rematch fight, she said, "I think Ben can finish him."

And, she's more than ready to get on the mat with her husband (she's remarried) for their BJJ classes. The mom of a champ said she's still young and needs to stay in shape. With her sons all grown up, she can selfishly live for herself.

She gets why her son Ben fights. It brings joy into his life. She can't ask for anything more as a mother.

She realizes she can't just be all work and no play; you've got to find something that brings joy in your life like her son, Ben. Happiness is temporary. Joy is a state of life, and it could be as simple as doing BJJ, even in your fifties. When you have joy in your life, you're doing things that feed the mind, body, and soul. Therefore, you are on your way to having that balanced life.

CPSIA information can be obtained at www.ICGtesting.com
Printed in the USA
LVOW101418101212

310853LV00003B/5/P